# IGNITING
# HOPE

*in 40 Days*

# IGNITING
# HOPE
## *in 40 Days*

## STEVE BACKLUND

ISBN: 978-1-7363601-3-2

# Acknowledgements

Editing: Ann Sutton Smith, Maxine Toh, Michelle Ragon, Brenna Yeary, and Shelter Musavengana

# Table of Contents

# About The Author

"Steve Backlund is known for his wisdom and practical insights on "how to do life." The students in our ministry school, Bethel School of Supernatural Ministry, love him because he always leaves them encouraged and refreshed in their vision. He has an unusual gift to take the mundane and make it exciting and to take the familiar and make it new."

*Bill Johnson, Bethel Church, Redding,*
*CA - Author of When Heaven Invades Earth*

If you enjoy this book, go to ignitinghope.com:

→ For blogs and podcasts
→ To purchase books and resources
→ For information on the Backlunds' speaking itinerary
→ To contact Steve or his wife, Wendy about speaking to your group
→ For many free resources to inspire your life
→ For online events to ignite your hope

## Other Books by Steve Backlund

*The Culture of Empowerment* - Whether you're a business owner, church small group leader, or family leader, the fastest way to make your vision for the future become a reality is to empower those you lead. This book shares Steve's lessons learned from raising up leaders around him.

*Igniting Faith in 40 Days* – Written with Wendy, this book is ideal for a 40-day negativity fast and to pour "spiritual gasoline" on your faith and hope.

*Cracks in the Foundation* – This writing examines the negative effects of religious tradition that neutralizes the power of God's promises. Its teachings will repair cracks in your faith foundation so God can build something great through you.

*Possessing Joy* – God has called us to serve Him with gladness. This book will give you incredible keys to do so.

*You're Crazy If You DON'T Talk to Yourself* – Life is in the power of the tongue. Jesus did not just *think* His way out of the wilderness, He *spoke truth* to invisible forces and to the mindsets that sought to restrict and defeat Him. This book will help you intentionally speak life over yourself.

*Victorious Mindsets* (Revised) – The power of intentional thinking. Steve Backlund reveals 50 biblical attitudes that are foundational for those who desire to walk in freedom and power.

# Introduction

I have invested much of my life to understand hope, experience hope, and share hope with others. Hope is the belief the future will be better than the present, and we have the power to help make it so. Hope is an overall optimistic attitude about the future based on the goodness and promises of God.

It would be difficult to over-emphasize the importance of hope. It gives us a reason to get up every morning, and I believe, after love, it is the most important quality for influence and catalytic leadership.

Hope is not just a perspective we can have in life, but, more importantly, hope is who God is. "Now may the God of hope fill you…" (Romans 15:13). One of my favorite worship songs is "Endless Ocean" by Jonathan David and Melissa Helser. It proclaims that there is no limit in what we can discover about God. Here is an excerpt:

> In my sin, You kept loving
> There's no end to Your forgiveness, and mercy
> Every morning, You keep coming
> Waves of Your affection, keep washing over me
>
> You are an endless ocean
> A bottomless sea
>
> All those angels, they are swimming
> In this ocean and they still can find no shore

Day and night, night and day
They keep seeing new sides of Your face

You are an endless ocean
A bottomless sea

There is no limit to the amount of God's love, forgiveness, power, wisdom and HOPE we can experience. It is indeed an endless ocean of goodness to be possessed. *Igniting Hope in 40 Days* contains my most recent discoveries about our God of hope and how to increase our hope levels dramatically. I've also included some of my favorite foundational truths and stories that set the course of my hope journey over twenty-five years ago.

These revelations have been an enormous well of hope to me. I bless you as you read and experience the transformational power of biblical optimism.

# I Am Repenting to Glistening Hope

*"Now may the God of hope fill you with all joy and peace in believing,*
*that you may abound in hope by the power of the Holy Spirit"*
                                                              *- Romans 15:13*

As a young pastor, I remember reading the words "glistening hope" in Francis Frangipane's book *The Three Battlegrounds*. He was describing our need for "glistening hope" saying that if we lack hope in an aspect of life, then we're believing a lie there and that area is in danger of having a stronghold of the enemy.

This truth rocked my world. I did not have much hope in my life and certainly not "glistening hope." **I was being set up for a great journey into the importance of hope that would change my life.** I asked the Lord to show me areas in my thinking where I was believing lies instead of truth. If a lack of hope meant evidence of lies, my low hope-meter meant there were plenty of lies to uncover.

Paul writes in Romans that "we also glory in tribulations, knowing that tribulation produces perseverance; and perseverance, character; and character, hope" (Romans 5:3-4). This passage encouraged me as I recognized tribulations lead us to Christian maturity. First, we "glory" (rejoice) in tribulation. Secondly, we continue (persevere) in this glorying. Third, we grow in Christian character (making good decisions). One would think that this character is the ultimate goal in Christian living, but it isn't.

**Our goal is ultimately hope: the confident expectation that good is coming.** Our destination is not good actions, but a way of thinking called hope. It is the soil that faith and obedience put their roots into. Without hope, there can be little lasting positive change.

"Repent, for the kingdom of God is at hand." Repentance is a change of thinking that leads to a change in actions. It is not a one-time event, but a lifestyle. We will know that our repentance in an area is complete when we consistently have glistening hope based on our revelation of God's goodness. My discouraging revelation of the lies I was believing gave me a choice: I could stay discouraged, or I could repent and change the foundations of my thinking in order to start on the path to true hope.

The steps to lie-removal and hope-building start with our conclusions. Lies typically don't start with facts but with our interpretation of those facts. **I came to realize that my conclusions about a circumstance were more important than the circumstance itself.** Moses sent out twelve spies for forty days in Numbers 13 to explore the Promised Land. When they came back, the spies were divided with two different conclusions about what they saw. One group (Joshua and Caleb) said "we can overcome this" and the other ten spies said they could not. The former experienced the promises, while the latter never saw fulfilment.

Once we see the importance of our conclusions, we begin to catch ourselves as non-hopeful conclusions start to creep in. As we mistrust these hope-deficient beliefs, we take the first step into overcoming the lies that bind us. Our hopelessness about a problem is almost always a bigger problem than the problem. If we try to change behaviors and circumstances without first addressing the beliefs creating a lack of hope, we likely won't see long-lasting transformation. When we tackle bad beliefs, it's amazing how our behaviors and circumstances start to change.

**The kingdom of God moves forward primarily by what we believe, not by what we do.** "Glistening hope" is a kingdom way of thinking that is foundational for having victorious mindsets.

Declarations:

1. I have a supernatural ability to spot lies and replace them with truth
2. I abound in hope through the power of the Holy Spirit
3. Because of a revelation of God's goodness toward me, every area of my life glistens with hope

# Problems are Opportunities to See How Big God Is

*"...all things work together for good to those who love God..."*
*- Romans 8:28*

In 2 Peter 1:4, it says that we have been given exceedingly great and precious promises. Through these promises, we might participate in the divine nature and a supernatural life. One of the greatest of these promises is Romans 8:28:

"And we know that all things work together for good to those who love God, to those who are the called according to His purpose."

This scripture has special meaning to all of us. It says that whatever happens to us, whether it is a choice we made or something out of our control, God can turn it to incredible good when we commit ourselves to His purpose. This applies to difficult childhoods, addictive behaviors, things that happen to us or around us, things happening in our nation, and many more. What a blessing!

In general, this scripture brings hope that something good is going to happen! What would happen if we tried "working out" this belief in life? My vision is that the world would catch hold of the passion to work out our beliefs and that this passion would exceed even the discipline of exercising our physical bodies. Bodily exercise is so important, and our physical, emotional, and mental health definitely profit from the workouts; but what if exercising our beliefs could be even more profitable to our overall health? What if exercising our beliefs has even more value because it also positively impacts our descendants?

I've been thinking about the mechanics of working out our beliefs. We understand from physical weight-lifting that, as we push against resistance, we build muscle and increase strength. What if the same thing holds true for our belief systems? Muscle is built in the spirit realm when we experience *resistance* against our joy, *resistance* against our dreams, *resistance* against our abundant life. Those struggles have something in them to help us.

Here is how you can start your own belief workouts. When you wake up in the morning, take an inventory of your emotions. When you find emotions like fear, worry, or frustration, realize you have resistance to build your belief muscles. Push against this resistance by speaking the promises of God related to the areas of concern in your life. Another key is to ask, "Lord, what are you doing in me that is connected to that?" "What can I extract out of this challenge in life or in my emotions?"

For example, what if you wake up in the morning and you feel like a failure? Maybe you have a situation in your life that says you are failing, but the Word says that you:

> ...are more than a conqueror
> ...will prosper in all things
> ...can do all things through Christ who strengthens you

By pressing against that negative feeling of failure, you have an opportunity to extract powerful good from that circumstance. You make war with scriptural truths. Resisting, then, actually strengthens your faith muscle.

One of the keys to successful living is to ask God these two questions:

- What are you doing in me that is related to the frustration, fear, or negative emotion that I am experiencing?
- What truth are You building in me as a vital key for my future?

Remember, there are no hopeless circumstances, there are only people who do not have hope. Once people get true hope, the circumstances can't stay the same.

Declarations:

1. I see divine opportunities in challenging situations and emotions I face
2. What God is doing in me is more important than what He is doing through me
3. I have a great plan to work out my beliefs daily

# There Are No Hopeless Situations: Part 1

*"...He who promised is faithful."*

*- Hebrews 10:23*

**S**omebody has overcome the very challenge you are facing right now. When we feed on testimonies of people coming out of great difficulty, it helps us believe we can too.

The Bible is full of people who overcame seemingly impossible situations. We have examples in our forerunners of faith to show us that we are not alone in feeling overwhelmed or discouraged when we face obstacles. Their stories remind us that just because something seems hopeless, doesn't mean it is.

**Here are some situations in the Bible that seemed hopeless but were not:**

**He Denied His Faith** – Peter said he would never deny Jesus, but he did–three times–right before Jesus was crucified. It would seem he squandered his destiny and now would have to settle for a life of regret and mediocrity. In the moment of his failure, Peter could easily have thought this would be his fate, but his worst fears did not happen. Peter was restored and became a key builder of the church in fulfillment of the prophetic word he received (Matthew 16:17-18).

**Her Husband Was Making Poor Choices** – Sarah had a husband who was wishy-washy and created dysfunction in her home. He gave in to her pressure to help God out by sleeping with Hagar (Sarah's handmaiden) resulting in the birth of Ishmael. Abraham lied twice in saying she was his sister which created huge messes. Their dream of a family of their own seemed out of reach for 100-year-old Abraham and 90-year-old Sarah, but it was not. After years of waiting and wondering if God's word would be fulfilled, the promise indeed came to pass. "And the Lord visited Sarah as He had said, and the Lord did for Sarah as He had spoken. For Sarah conceived and bore Abraham a son in his old age" (Genesis 21:1).

**Their City Was Heading Toward Judgment** – Ninevah was a wicked city; its inhabitants' sin was removing any remaining spiritual protection it had left, and judgment was imminent. To the citizens of the city, preservation seemed hopeless until a reluctant prophet named Jonah preached one message that sparked a city-wide spiritual revival and spared its people (See the Book of Jonah).

**He Had a Series of Tragedy and Pain** – Job could not understand what had happened. Tragedy had struck his family, his possessions, and his health. His "friends" made things worse by blaming him. He seemed destined to end his days in bitterness and misery–but no–his life turned around. "Now the Lord blessed the latter days of Job more than his beginning" (Job 42:12).

Each of these situations looked hopeless, but it was not. What an encouragement this is to us as we face seemingly insurmountable obstacles! The next devotional contains even more examples to ignite your hope.

---

Declarations:

1. My prayers are working powerfully even if don't see or feel they are
2. I have an unusual ability to have hope for people, nations, and for myself
3. I bring breakthrough and revival wherever I go

# There Are No Hopeless Situations: Part 2

*"...rejoicing in hope, patient in tribulation, continuing steadfastly in prayer..."*

- Romans 12:12

Continue to meditate today on testimonies that will encourage your spirit. Below are more stories of people who overcame seemingly hopeless situations:

**He Was Rejected by a Spiritual Father** – Mark was trying to be faithful, but the Apostle Paul removed him from his ministry team (Acts 15:39). Even though Mark continued to minister with Barnabas, Paul's negative opinion had the potential to greatly limit his ministry. Mark may have thought it was inevitable that this key influencer would always think less of him, but breakthrough came and Paul's opinion changed. In Paul's last epistle, he wrote this, "Get Mark and bring him with you, for he is useful to me for ministry" (2 Timothy 4:11).

**He Was an Influential Leader Who Was Suicidal** – Elijah was one of the greatest leaders of the Old Testament. He was chosen along with Moses to appear to Jesus on the Mount of Transfiguration. Even so, he was depressed and suicidal after he heard Jezebel wanted to kill him. Did he stay this way? No. After getting some rest, God said, "Go...anoint Hazael *as* king over Syria...anoint Jehu the son of Nimshi *as* king over Israel. And Elisha...you shall anoint *as* prophet in your place" (1 Kings 19:15-16). Elijah came out of his emotional struggle by clarifying his assignment and purpose for the next season.

**She Had a Series of Relationship Failures** – The woman at the well had been married five times and was now living with another man. It certainly would be unwise to have hope that she could be a significant revivalist. Or, would it? This unlikely woman became an evangelist to her town and a catalyst for the spread of the gospel in Samaria: "And many of the Samaritans of that city believed in Him because of the word of the woman who testified...They urged Him to stay with them, and He stayed there two days. And many more believed because of His own word" (John 4:39-41).

**He Was the Least Likely to Become a Christian** – Saul of Tarsus zealously persecuted Christians. How could someone like that ever get saved? "Impossible," many would say. But he did, and he became one of the greatest Christian influencers ever.

**His Commitment to Integrity and Purity Held Back His Dream**– Joseph resisted Potiphar's wife's advances and was put in prison for thirteen years. Instead of promoting him, his purity plan seemingly made life harder. "I have wasted my life," he could have thought. "God has forgotten me." That was not the end of the story because everything changed in one day. He interpreted Pharoah's dream and became second in command in Egypt (See Genesis 41).

There is hope even in the worst situations as illustrated in the nine biblical examples we have studied. No matter what you are facing today, God has delivered someone in the same situation before. Thank you, Father, you will do it again.

Declarations:

1. God does miracles in me, through me, and for me
2. The most influential and rewarding days of my entire lifetime are still ahead of me
3. I bring hope and breakthrough to others in seemingly impossible circumstances

# Overcoming Pessimism

*"Let us hold fast the confession of our hope..."*

*- Hebrews 10:23*

A pessimist has the tendency to emphasize negative aspects, conditions, and possibilities, or to expect the worst possible outcomes. Optimism is the opposite of this. In the classic water glass example, pessimists would say it is half empty while an optimist would call it half full.

People of hope are on a mission to overcome pessimism. Hope is an overall optimistic attitude about the future based on the goodness and promises of God. "Let us hold fast the confession of our hope without wavering, for He who promised is faithful" (Hebrews 10:23). **I am not a proponent of positive thinking but of biblical optimism.** Our hope level determines our influence level.

There are two ways to live. First, we can live a pessimistic life and never be disappointed. Or, we can live an optimistic, hope-filled life with occasional disappointment. It is this second option that sets us up for victory and influence.

Here are five ways to overcome pessimism:

1. **Recognize it** – Even though we will all experience occasional pessimistic feelings, it is not normal to create a personality out of them. In an effort to be "realistic", many are perpetually negative

and don't even know it. When we admit this tendency in our lives, we take the first step to overcoming it.

2. **Know its Source** – Pessimism is not a personality issue, it is a belief issue. "Now may the God of hope fill you...in believing" (Romans 15:13). Increasing hope is the evidence we are believing truth, while increasing pessimism is the evidence we are believing lies.

3. **Understand it is a Great Enemy** – The story of the twelve spies in Numbers 13 is enlightening. They spy out the Promised Land for 40 days and come back with their report. Ten of the spies brought a pessimistic conclusion, while Joshua and Caleb were optimistic. This tells us that our conclusions about a situation are often more important than the situation itself. A chronic negative bent in our conclusions is a great enemy of God's purposes.

4. **Attack it with Truth** – David "encouraged himself in the Lord" in 1 Samuel 30:6. His family had just been kidnapped, his city had been burned, and his soldiers wanted to kill him, but he overcame his hopelessness. I believe he spoke God's promises over himself as a means to shift his perspective.

5. **Set Others Free from it** – When we regularly share our own journey of becoming more hopeful, or when we engage in something like a book reading club on radical mind renewal, we create a situation where we will be regularly confronted with what we need to hear ourselves. This increases our level of personal victory, and we get to help others as well.

Our optimism does not mean we will encourage every choice people consider. People of hope are people of firm conviction. As we fix our minds on God's promises and determine to live in possibility and not pessimism, we position ourselves to receive His goodness in higher levels than we've ever known before.

Declarations:

1. I walk in high-level biblical optimism
2. I am overcoming the lies that would create pessimism in me
3. I am a Joshua and a Caleb to this generation

# Celebrate Progress, Not Perfection

*"...He who has begun a good work in you will complete it..."*
*- Philippians 1:6*

C elebrating progress is part of having a hope-filled outlook on life. It is always fun to celebrate a toddler who is learning to walk, even though he is falling down more than he is walking. We don't withhold approval from him until perfect walking is achieved, but we cheer on this child who is growing in the gift of walking.

Even though I would celebrate a baby's progress, I noticed I would not celebrate my own progress in personal areas of growth. This negative tendency resulted from my upbringing but was greatly increased by a religious mindset.

Under a religious mindset, we can't be joyful or celebrate until there is perfection. Religious, perfectionist, performance-based mindsets tend to only celebrate perfection, but families celebrate progress. We are the family of God, and the celebration of progress is part of family life (even for ourselves).

Here are five biblically-supported celebrations to help you build a hope-filled outlook on life:

1. **The Process Celebration** – "As newborn babes, desire the pure milk of the word, that you may grow thereby" (1 Peter 2:2). We are likened to babies here, and we are told our spiritual growth

26

is a normal process. It is God's plan for us to do things better and better as we mature.

2. **The Delighting in the Lord Celebration** – "Delight yourself also in the Lord, and He shall give you the desires of your heart" (Psalm 37:4). It is difficult to delight in the Lord if we are not delighting in ourselves. Those who go on the journey to truly delight in the Lord will have to overcome negativity toward themselves.

3. **The "He is a Good Completer" Celebration** – "Being confident of this very thing, that He who has begun a good work in you will complete *it* until the day of Jesus Christ" (Philippians 1:6). Our faith ought not to be in our own ability to grow but in His ability to finish what He has started in us. This verse is one of the greatest reasons to celebrate our progress.

4. **The Worshipping Glory to Glory Celebration** – "But we all, with unveiled face, beholding as in a mirror the glory of the Lord, are being transformed into the same image from glory to glory, just as by the Spirit of the Lord" (2 Corinthians 3:18). As we really see Him, we will become increasingly like him (moving from glory to glory). We cannot truly behold Him if we are burdened down with a "veiled face" of guilt, condemnation, and self-disapproval.

5. **The Building Spiritual Muscle Celebration** – "Not that I have already attained, or am already perfected; but I press on, that I may lay hold of that for which Christ Jesus has also laid hold of me. Brethren, I do not count myself to have apprehended; but one thing *I do,* forgetting those things which are behind and reaching forward to those things which are ahead. I press toward the goal for the prize of the upward call of God in Christ Jesus" (Philippians 3:12-14). It is interesting Paul said he is not perfected yet. He pressed against resistance in his life to keep growing his spiritual muscles. We too can celebrate when it feels hard to get to a higher level (our upward calls in life).

These are powerful verses to propel us to radically celebrate ourselves. As we celebrate our progress, instead of waiting for perfection to do so, we will find hope and joy growing in us which will strengthen and improve our lives in incredible ways.

Declarations:

1. I have an unusual ability to celebrate progress—not perfection— in my life and in the lives of others
2. I am like a kid in a candy shop eagerly waiting to see the good things God has for me
3. I love life and overflow with enthusiasm for who I am and what I do

# More Reasons to Celebrate Your Progress

*"...the joy of the LORD is your strength."* - Nehemiah 8:10

Remember, just as we celebrate a toddler who is making progress learning to walk, we are to celebrate our own progress. With toddlers, we focus on what they are doing well, instead of dwelling on what they are not doing. The same strategy will work well in learning to step into new areas of growth in our lives. Our gifts will get stronger.

Why don't we normally celebrate progress?

1. **We might believe that if we don't use guilt and condemnation to motivate ourselves, we might think we are okay and stop improving.** However, these negative motivational tools will not have a lasting positive effect.

2. **We may fear that celebration would only lead to pride.** Pride doesn't mean you think you're great; it means that you think you are greater than other people. We all need to celebrate the growing greatness in us as we "arise and shine for our light has come" (Isaiah 60).

3. **We also might believe God is not celebrating what we're doing, so why should we?** (Galatians 5) God celebrates that Jesus died and took our place. Just as God celebrated Jesus on earth, He celebrates those who believe in Jesus right now.

Here are five momentous reasons for celebrating progress:

1. **It opens your eyes to where grace is manifesting in your life** (Philippians 1:6). Let's focus on this truth again. Paul is confident that He who has begun a good work in you will complete it until the day of Jesus Christ. I don't have faith in my ability to perform well, I have faith in God's ability to complete what He started in and through me.

2. **It helps silence the accuser's voice of condemnation toward you** (Revelation 12:10; Romans 8:1). The accuser is cast down and, in Jesus, there is no more condemnation. One of the greatest weapons the enemy has is to tell you who you are not. As we celebrate progress in who we are, we silence the enemy.

3. **It creates momentum in your life and something to build on for the future** (Philippians 3:12-14). When David confronted Goliath, he rehearsed his victories and celebrated his progress. As he did, he gained momentum for the battle that he was facing at that moment. We can celebrate simple things like, "Wow! I didn't get frustrated as quickly this week with my co-worker." Try it, and you'll start to break negative cycles and create positive growth trajectories.

4. **It increases the joy of the Lord in your life** (Nehemiah 8:10; Proverbs 17:22). As we see the joy of grandparents watching toddlers learn to walk, we can understand the atmosphere of encouragement in which we are designed to thrive. We need strength in the middle of the journey, not at the end. Try encouraging yourself in the middle of the journey toward your goals, and see strength build through joy.

5. **It will increase your celebration of others** (Hebrews 10:24). Love your neighbor as you love yourself. If we celebrate our own progress, we will celebrate the progress of others. We will notice and celebrate the good things that they are doing. We are called to speak life and encourage others.

Try having a conversation with God today about all of the things He celebrates you for in the past week, month, or year. You'll be surprised how long your list is and how good and hope-filled you feel about yourself and your relationship with the Lord afterward!

Declarations:

1. I continually celebrate the things that are right with me
2. Like David, I remember the "lion(s) and the bear(s)" I have killed
3. I celebrate myself and others

# Promises That Ignite Biblical Optimism

*"Let us hold fast the confession of our hope..."* - Hebrews 10:23

I am not a proponent of positive thinking, but I am a proclaimer of biblical optimism. Hebrews 10:23 tells us why: "Let us hold fast the confession of *our* hope without wavering, for He who promised *is* faithful."

Our hope increases when we believe truth. "Now may the God of hope fill you with all joy and peace in believing, that you may abound in hope by the power of the Holy Spirit" (Romans 15:13). Our hope level is the indicator of whether we are believing lies or truth.

Something powerful happens when we believe the truth of God's promises. "By which have been given to us exceedingly great and precious promises, that through these you may be partakers of the divine nature" (2 Peter 1:4). We do not automatically experience the promises of God; they are brought into our lives by renewing our minds with them (Romans 12:2). One of the main ways to renew our minds with God's promises is to declare them.

Below are five promises to declare that will ignite biblical optimism. Your hope and faith will rise as you speak them out loud.

1.  **The Promise of Supernatural Ability** – "I can do all things through Christ who strengthens me" (Philippians 4:13). "Thank you, Father, that I have supernatural abilities in relationships, in my choices, in my influence, and in all things."

2. **The Promise of Supernatural Completion** – "Being confident of this very thing, that He who has begun a good work in you will complete *it* until the day of Jesus Christ" (Philippians 1:6). "Thank You, Father, that You are completing what you have started in me, in my family, my nation, and in the world."

3. **The Promise of Supernatural Restoration** – "And we know that all things work together for good to those who love God, to those who are the called according to *His* purpose" (Romans 8:28). "Thank You, Father, that everything in my past is being turned into an incredibly positive thing for me right now and in my future."

4. **The Promise of Supernatural Provision** – "And my God shall supply all your needs according to His riches in glory by Christ Jesus" (Philippians 4:19). "Thank You, Father, that You are providing my spiritual needs, my emotional needs, my financial needs, my relational needs, my family needs, my ministry needs, my city's needs, and my nation's needs."

5. **The Promise of Supernatural Solutions** – "No temptation has overtaken you except what is common to mankind. And God is faithful; He will not let you be tempted beyond what you can bear. But when you are tempted, He will also provide a way out so that you can endure it" (1 Corinthians 10:13). "Thank You, Father, that there are divine solutions manifesting for every challenge and every divinely inspired dream in my life."

As you take time to personalize your declarations for these five promises, you will increase your biblical optimism, plus you will increasingly see the divine nature manifest in you and around you.

Declarations:

1. My future is as bright as the promises of God
2. I have an unusual grace to believe and activate God's promises in my life
3. I always have hope because I know God is faithful and His promises are true

# God is Working Even When We Don't See It

*"For we walk by faith, not by sight."*

*- 2 Corinthians 5:7*

It's not working! All of us at times are tempted to conclude this in our Christian walk. We look for proof that God is working in key areas, and we think, "He's not moving!" Or we think we've done all the right things and still don't see the results we expected.

Many in the Bible had situations where things did not seem to be working. Here are three:

- Abraham and Sarah's promised child had not come despite years of waiting
- Joseph's purity seemed to only make things worse as he ended up in jail
- Elijah's radical obedience in defeating the prophets of Baal led to a season where he became suicidal because of the opposition he faced

When it does not seem to be working, it is wise to ask God what He is really doing in us. Delays deepen our character, which ultimately causes us to be able to keep the increased blessing He is bringing. Here are eight things God might be doing in us when it seems like it is not working:

1. **You are learning to love the promise giver more than the promise** – "(God) is a rewarder of those who diligently seek

Him" (Hebrews 11:6). When we are more interested in seeking His face than His hand, we are then positioned for the increase.

2. **You are being called to think bigger** – Many times we think too small. We can be so frustrated with a door that is not opening that we cannot see the bigger doors that will open.

3. **You are embracing a season of living by faith, not sight** – "For we walk by faith, not by sight" (2 Corinthians 5:7). All of us need to be weaned from getting our beliefs from what we see instead of what we know.

4. **You are seeing God's need and committing to it** – It wasn't working for a frustrated Hannah in I Samuel 1 until she connected her need with God's need. When she understood God's need for a prophet and gave herself to that, the breakthrough happened.

5. **You are overcoming the victim mindset** – "Tell my people to move forward" (Exodus 14:15). The children of Israel felt helpless at the edge of the Red Sea. As they overcame the victim mindset and moved forward, the sea parted. Overcomers find ways to keep moving forward in life even when there seems to be major unfulfilled promises in their lives.

6. **Your eyes are being opened to what you already have** – The widow in 2 Kings 4 realized her solution was something she already had (the oil). There is something we currently have that God will use supernaturally.

7. **You are learning not to quit** – "We will reap if we faint not" (Galatians 6:9). Perseverance and endurance are incredible qualities to develop.

8. **You are in a season of embracing your worth in Christ** – We are only able to receive what we think we are worth in areas like favor, finances, and authority. If we are blessed beyond what we think we are worth, we will often self-sabotage our lives back to the level we believe we are worth. As we accept our worth in

Christ, it will promote more breakthrough than all the Christian formulas we have.

When we think it is not working, God invites us to ask for wisdom (James 1:5). He will answer us with one of the above perspectives or something else. Once we believe we have heard from Him, we can confidently proclaim, "He is working! He is moving!" And, you know what? He really is.

Declarations:

1. Even when I don't see it or feel it, God is working powerfully in my life
2. I have incredible insight into what God is doing in me when I experience delays in seeing His promises manifest
3. I help others gain wisdom and receive breakthrough faith in their seasons of delayed promises

# Wake Up to Good Beliefs

*"Set your mind on things above, not on things on the earth."*
*- Colossians 3:2*

My wife Wendy's first question to herself each morning used to be, "How do I feel today?" She realized this was not the question to ask. The better question is, "What do I believe today?" She began to understand if she wanted a different emotion, she needed to have a different belief. (She expands on this in her great book *Victorious Emotions*.)

**The kingdom of God is not moved forward by good conduct but by good beliefs.** The Old Covenant was advanced by focusing on behavior (the law), but the New Covenant is propelled by believing truth. This is confirmed by the Apostle Paul's rebuke of the Galatians for not understanding this:

> "O foolish Galatians! Who has bewitched you that you should not obey the truth...This only I want to learn from you: Did you receive the Spirit by the works of the law, or by the hearing of faith? **Are you so foolish? Having begun in the Spirit, are you now being made perfect by the flesh?...**Therefore He who supplies the Spirit to you and works miracles among you, *does He do it* by the works of the law, or by the hearing of faith?" (Galatians 3:1-5).

**The way we get into the kingdom is the same way we advance in it.** What is this way? It is by hearing the good news of the gospel and believing it. We are called "Believers," and this should tip us off to what we are to prioritize.

**Paul says we are "in the flesh" if we are primarily trying to grow by focusing on the works of the law (our conduct and behavior).** When we wait for our feelings to tell us what is true, we bypass our spiritual promises and rely on the flesh. Being in the flesh stunts our growth and limits our effectiveness because, in the flesh, we base our perspective on what is currently happening, rather than what we believe about the nature and promises of God.

Meditation on these promises is key to a life in the spirit, and the Bible is full of them. One of my favorites is The Promise of Supernatural Restoration: "And we know that all things work together for good to those who love God, to those who are the called according to His purpose" (Romans 8:28). With this renewed perspective, we can see potential despite our circumstances and say, "Thank You, Father, that everything in my past is being turned into an incredibly positive thing for me right now and in my future."

With a foundation of clear biblical promises, I recommend declaring some or all of the "25 Declarations to Increase Influence and Leadership" that you can find on our blog. Here are five examples from this list to start your day believing strong.

1. Adaptability – *I will thrive no matter what happens*
2. Solutions – *In every situation I face, I have many* options*, solutions, and divine ideas. There is always a solution*
3. "Bottom-Lining" – *Even if the worst happens, I will be okay*
4. Identity – *I am not who my past says I am; I am who God says I am*
5. Valuing Process – *I don't wait for perfection to celebrate myself and be joyful*

Let's follow Wendy's example when we wake up and ask, "What do I believe today?"

Declarations:

1. The kingdom of God is primarily moved forward not by good works but by good beliefs
2. In the morning and throughout the day, I focus more on what I believe than what I feel
3. I am a person of incredible beliefs who inspires others to believe truth instead of lies

# Magnify God, Not the Problem

*"Oh, magnify the LORD with me..."*

*- Psalm 34:3*

Psalm 34 contains incredible wisdom about how to walk in hope. In this devotional, we focus on verses one to four:

> I will bless the Lord at all times;
> His praise *shall* continually *be* in my mouth.
> My soul shall make its boast in the Lord;
> The humble shall hear *of it* and be glad.
> **Oh, magnify the Lord with me,**
> **And let us exalt His name together.**
> I sought the Lord, and He heard me,
> And delivered me from all my fears (Psalm 34:1-4).

I have highlighted Verse 3, "Oh, magnify the Lord with me." When we magnify something, we make it appear bigger. The Psalmist David desired to create an environment with other people which would cause them to see God as bigger, greater, more powerful, and more faithful than ever before. Wow! What a desire. And it is amazing to realize that no matter how much we magnify Him, we will never get close to how big and great He really is.

**Yes, we have the ability to magnify God, but we also have the ability to magnify our problems and make them bigger than they really are.** This is what the ten spies did in Numbers 13. Their unbelief and unhealthy verbal processing of their scouting experience skewed their perception of the giants' size and limited how much of God's promises they experienced. What we focus on magnifies. As they enlarged their difficulties with their words and attention, they made God smaller in their eyes. On the contrary, Joshua and Caleb magnified the Lord together, saw the obstacle in its proper size, and eventually entered the Promised Land.

**These habits will magnify your problems:**

1. Speaking everything you feel
2. Feeding on bad news and the perspectives of pessimists
3. Spending most of your time with people who have victim mindsets

**These habits will magnify the Lord in your life:**

1. Fully participating in victory-based worship in song
2. Regularly speaking and meditating on God's promises
3. Consuming testimonies of breakthrough, healing, deliverance, salvation, provision, and miracles. Downloading the Increase Testimony App on your smartphone will help greatly with this. (iPhone: http://bit.ly/increasetestimony or Android: https://bit. ly/gp-increasetestimony)
4. Engaging in deep fellowship with others where there is authenticity, discussing Scripture, prayer, and risk taking

In closing, these words from Philippians will greatly help us magnify the Lord. "Be anxious for nothing, but in everything by prayer and supplication, with thanksgiving, let your requests be made known to God; and the peace of God, which surpasses all understanding, will guard your hearts and minds through Christ Jesus. Finally, brethren, whatever things are true, whatever things *are* noble, whatever things *are* just, whatever things *are* pure, whatever things *are* lovely, whatever things *are* of good report, if *there is* any virtue and if *there is* anything praiseworthy—meditate on these things." (Philippians 4:6-8).

Declarations:

1. I magnify the Lord, not my problems
2. I create environments and atmospheres where whole groups of people magnify the Lord and, through this, nations are changed
3. I am a Joshua and a Caleb to this generation

# Go Against the Flow of Unbelief

*"...reaching forward to those things which are ahead..."*
*- Philippians 3:13*

"Not that I have already attained, or am already perfected; but I press on, that I may lay hold of that for which Christ Jesus has also laid hold of me. Brethren, I do not count myself to have apprehended; but one thing *I do,* forgetting those things which are behind and reaching forward to those things which are ahead, I press toward the goal for the prize of the upward call of God in Christ Jesus" (Philippians 3:12-14).

Weight lifters understand that muscles are built by pressing against resistance. Overcoming Christians also understand that resistance is a friend in our journey to become fully convinced about God's goodness and His promises.

**Salmon are fascinating fish.** They are birthed in fresh water, then live in the ocean for years, and finally come back to fresh water to spawn so that their species can increase in number. The remarkable thing about this process is that they spawn in the same location where they were born, and they often overcome great odds to get there. **God has put in them a directional homing device and an overcoming spirit to fulfill their calling. He has done the same for us.**

"For this is the love of God, that we keep His commandments. And His commandments are not burdensome. For whatever is born of God overcomes the world. And this is the victory that has overcome the world—our faith" (1 John 5:2-4). We also have what it takes to press against resistance in order to move forward. Truly, the victorious Christian will embrace a life of swimming upstream against old "mind currents" that want to imprison him or her in valleys of unfruitfulness. One way to do this is by setting the course of our lives with words to resist the flow of unbelief.

Here are some common situations that often contain lies, which can be combated with a specific promise of God:

1. **When experiencing lack and uncertainty, say**, "My God shall supply all my needs according to His riches in glory" (Philippians 4:19)

2. **When feeling hopeless, say**, "God has a way to get me from here to where I need to be. There is a direction for me to take that is powerful and good, and He will empower me to walk in it" (1 Corinthians 10:13)

3. **When feeling weak, say**, "I can do all things through Him who strengthens me" (Philippians 4:13)

4. **When you think you are a failure, say**, "He who has begun a good work in me will complete it" (Philippians 1:6)

5. **When you don't know what else to do, bottom line things and say**, "I am going to be okay because my God will make things work out for me" (Romans 8:28)

These responses will help us set the course of our lives toward God's Promised Land and away from mediocre living. There have been seasons in my life where I have had to devote extra time to speaking and thinking God's promises. Remember, His promises allow us "to participate in the divine nature" of supernatural living (2 Peter 1:4).

Spoken words have a powerful effect, but inner self talk is also important. We resist lies first in our thoughts. Remember, you might be crazy if you don't talk to yourself. (More on this topic is available in my book *You're Crazy If You Don't Talk to Yourself.*)

Declarations:

1. My God DNA causes me to overcome obstacles on my journey to my highest inner victory and purpose
2. I understand and strategically deploy the promises of God to see breakthrough and transformation
3. As I speak my biblical identity and God's promises, I am propelled into incredible victory and influence

# Why You Can Be Radically Encouraged Now

*"...be transformed by the renewing of your mind..."*
- Romans 8:28

Our ministry's core message affirms the believer's birthright to overflowing hope and joy, and proclaims the strategy of godly mind renewal (Romans 12:2) to experience the radical fulfillment and victory that come from right believing. Though many are encouraged by these truths, the process of establishing new strongholds of hope in your mind can be a journey that takes time. Just as athletes need to be reminded of their vision and to celebrate progress in the midst of difficult and exhausting training, so do you as you do the work to establish new thought patterns and beliefs.

Kris Vallotton often preaches, "Vision gives pain a purpose." In light of this, here are seven reasons for you to be overflowing with thanksgiving and hope even in the midst of your mind renewal journey; reasons you can be radically encouraged not only at the end of the journey, but right *now.*

1. **There is no one like you** – You and your calling are entirely unique and no one can fulfill it like you. There is no one on the planet who is wired and designed just like you, and who has had the experiences in life you've had. You can powerfully reach people that few others can.

2. **Many have overcome the challenges you're currently facing** – Whether you're battling personal, relational, financial, or circumstantial obstacles, be encouraged that multitudes have overcome the same thing and lived a life of purpose and fulfillment.

3. **Your biggest challenge is not about you** – James 1:12 says that a "crown of life" is given to those who overcome. This crown represents authority to impart life and breakthrough to others in the same area which has been overcome. Your greatest struggle right now is equipping you with compassion and power to impart victory and strategies to others for the same battle.

4. **Your past is being turned to good** – "All things work for good for those who love God and are called according to His purpose," (Romans 8:28). As we prioritize our relationship with God, *ALL* things from our past are working for our good. This is especially encouraging when we consider negative things that have happened in our lives.

5. **You are increasing your load-bearing capacity** – God's purpose is for us to move toward greater kingdom influence in our families, our communities, our nations, and beyond. In order to have greater influence, we need a greater load-bearing capacity. Both physical and emotional muscles are built by pushing against resistance. Your current difficult circumstances and emotions are opportunities to increase your load-bearing capacity for the great callings on your life in the days ahead.

6. **You are storing up treasure in heaven** – Jesus calls us to do this in Matthew 6:19. As we think from an eternal perspective, we realize that there is much more to life than just having good circumstances here on earth.

7. **God's promises are true** – "Let us hold fast the confession of our hope without wavering, for He who promised is faithful," (Hebrews 10:23). Ultimately, our encouragement comes from believing that God is faithful and His promises are true. As we declare biblical promises, we will be encouraged.

Today is a great day to be encouraged! These seven realities will make a difference for you and those you share them with.

Declarations:

1. I am encouraged today because God's promises are working in my life
2. Because I encourage myself radically, I am able to encourage others in incredible, life-changing ways
3. The truths of this devotional are changing my life

# Change Your Self-Talk With These Five Phrases

*"Death and life are in the power of the tongue..."*

*- Proverbs 18:21*

By Wendy Backlund

Whether we're aware of it or not, we're continually communicating to ourselves. We internally and verbally relay messages to our spirits of either hope and encouragement or death and discouragement all day long through our self-talk. Proverbs 18:21 says "Life and death are in the power of the tongue." It's amazing how we can shift and bring life to our emotions and the state of our physical bodies just by speaking something truth-filled and different, which also causes us to think something different. Take time today to notice your self-talk and how it affects you.

For instance, one self-defeating phrase we often tell ourselves is, "I *have* to do X today." Without realizing it, you will probably feel a heaviness or dread attached to that task because you're communicating it as something you're begrudgingly required to do. Instead, try switching it up from "I have to" and say **"I *get* to do X today."** Speak it out loud, and your body will respond with increased anticipation and energy toward that task.

Another energy-draining phrase we commonly tell ourselves is "This is hard." When we say this and agree with this idea, our bodies and our emotions respond negatively with overwhelmed feelings and a desire to quit. In these instances, instead say out loud, **"This is easy and fun!"**

Say it like you mean it, and you will begin to feel a shift occur within you. Your creativity and confidence will begin to flow again.

Here are three more phrases that are great to say to yourself everyday to help your body function at its best and to help you maintain your joy:

- **"My best is more than enough."** This is one of my favorite phrases. I try to keep these words dancing in my head all day so I am less likely to feel self-doubt or fear of failure. I use this declaration to remind myself that I am co-laboring with God and the unseen realm, therefore everything I do is touched by the supernatural.

- **"I love moving my body."** I use this when I don't get a good parking space near the door, or when my body feels tired or achy, and wants to give up. Parents, this is also a great tool when you've just sat down for a moment and one of the kids needs you to do something for them again.

- **"I am excited to do this."** When we say things like "I have to go to the meeting, instead of "I get to go to the meeting," we unconsciously deplete our energy. Sports teams are our example of how using victorious and enthusiastic words creates energy before they play their games.

We all have self-talk continually running in our minds. Begin to become aware of how your own thoughts affect your emotions and your body. Intentionally creating new, life-giving phrases in your self-talk will guide you towards a healthier and happier you.

Declarations:

1. I have a supernatural grace to think energizing and life-giving thoughts and to speak energizing and life-giving words
2. My self-talk is full of hope and joy
3. I have a unique ability to help others to overcome self-limiting beliefs and negative self-talk

# Change The Channel

*"Now may the God of hope fill you with all joy and peace in believing..."*

*- Romans 15:13*

Radios are incredible machines—they have the ability to tune into communication that is already in the atmosphere. Just like the natural realm, the spirit realm has communications we can tune into that will influence our self-talk. Frequently, many of us accidentally tune into the wrong channels in the spirit, like:

- "The accuser of the brethren" channel
- "You are who your past says you are" channel
- "Don't get your hopes up" channel
- "You are a victim" channel

**But God has life-giving, identity-releasing channels for you. How do we know if we are listening to the wrong channel?** We can check ourselves with a quick hope self-test. If what we are listening to doesn't give us hope for ourselves, for others, for our nation, or for our circumstances, then we are listening to the wrong channel.

Also, if our interpretation of Scripture doesn't give us hope, then we are listening to the wrong channel in how we interpret the Bible. For example, we can perceive the Bible from an old covenant perspective that causes us to fear punishment. We can listen to the "you've been disappointed" channel, and our past hurts can also cause us to interpret the Bible in a flawed manner.

**If we're not interpreting Scripture with hope, we're listening to the wrong channel.**

Romans 15:13 says, "Now may the God of hope fill you with all joy and peace in believing that you may abound in hope by the power of the Holy Spirit." The moment we believe truth and properly interpret the Bible we should abound in hope; it should overflow from our mouths as our first response.

In Hebrews 10:23, we're reminded to "...hold fast to the confession of our hope without wavering, for He who promised is faithful." It tells us that the more we believe God is faithful, the more hope-filled we will be. I'm not into positive thinking, I'm into biblical optimism.

There are so many people in the Bible that changed channels in the spirit to hear something else. Gideon was listening to the victim channel, the "it's too late" channel, the "I'm stuck" channel, and the "I've got to protect myself" channel. But he chose to tune into something different when the angel of the Lord began speaking identity over him, calling him a "mighty man of valor." Jacob was also listening to the wrong channel in Genesis 32 when he wrestled with the angel, saying he wouldn't let the angel go until he blessed him. This blessing was a revelation that his name and identity would be changed from "deceiver" (Jacob) to "Prince with God" (Israel).

Are the channels you're listening to giving you hope? If not, some channel adjustments need to be made.

Listen to these stations instead to restore your hope based on God's truth and His perspective:

- "Your true biblical identity" channel (Philippians 4:13)
- "You are not who your past says you are" channel (2 Corinthians 5:17)

- "You are forgiven and in right-standing with God" channel (2 Corinthians 5:21)
- "God will finish what He started in you" channel (Philippians 1:6)

God is going to change and grow what needs to be changed in you.

**You have a future and a hope because vision for the future gives power and purpose for the present.**

God is helping you to recognize any stations you may be tuned into that are robbing you of your true identity and God's perspective of your life. You can do it. Tune in to that which gives you hope.

Declarations:

1. My self-talk is filled with hope because I believe what God has said
2. I do not trust any thought or conclusion in my life which does not have hope attached to it
3. I inspire and equip others to think incredible hope-filled thoughts, leading them to influence the world in astounding ways

# Staying on the Right Channel

*"...whatever things are of good report...meditate on these things."*
*- Philippians 4:8*

We learned in the last devotional that we know we are listening to the wrong channel if what we hear does not give us hope. Even when God corrects us there will be hope. "Now may the God of hope fill you...in believing" (Romans 15:13).

Here are five keys to keep you on the right channel in your self-talk:

1.  **Take care of yourself** – "Elijah said, 'It is enough! Now, Lord, take my life...' Then...suddenly an angel touched him, and said to him, 'Arise *and* eat'" (1 Kings 19:4-5). Even though he had just experienced a major supernatural victory against the prophets of Baal, now he was afraid and suicidal—tuned into the wrong channel. God's solution is simple: "Eat something." Some of our negative self-talk stems from lack of rest, inadequate exercise, or poor nutrition. We can often feed our hope by taking care of our physical needs.

2.  **Move forward** – "And the Lord said to Moses, 'Why do you cry to Me? Tell the children of Israel to go forward'" (Exodus 14:15). As they moved forward, they saw breakthrough. Is there an area in which you can trust God by taking the first step forward?

3. **Utilize the power of "thank you"** – "Be anxious for nothing, but in everything by prayer and supplication, *with thanksgiving, let your requests be made known to God; and the peace of God, which surpasses all understanding, will guard your hearts and minds through Christ Jesus*" (Philippians 4:6-7). We stay on God's peace channel when we utilize the power of thanksgiving. "Thank you, Father, that you are meeting my needs, moving in my family, turning all things to good in my life, and giving me great clarity in decision making."

4. **Feed on testimonies of what God is doing** – "Finally, brethren, whatever things are true, whatever things *are* noble, whatever things *are* just, whatever things *are* pure, whatever things *are* lovely, whatever things *are* of good report, if *there is* any virtue and if *there is* anything praiseworthy—meditate on these things" (Philippians 4:8). My pastor, Bill Johnson, regularly feeds on God's faithfulness (Psalm 37:3) and relentlessly directs us to exchange testimonies of what God has done in order to keep us on the right channel.

5. **Celebrate progress, not perfection** – Perfectionism causes us to tune in to the "you are a failure" channel. Just as we celebrate a toddler's one step, we are wise to celebrate the little improvements we make.

One of the greatest revelations we can get is that we have the power to think joyfully, peacefully, and hopefully. You will discover and practice how to tune in to God's channels of hope. My book, *You're Crazy If You Don't Talk to Yourself,* is a great resource for changing our self-talk, speaking to ourselves with grace, power, and kindness, and harnessing the power of declarations.

Declarations:

1. My self-talk is full of hope because I believe God's promises are true
2. I do not trust any thought in my life which does not glisten with hope
3. God's grace and power cause me to believe like Jesus did in the gospels

# Defeating the Crippling Effects of Perfectionism

*"...He has perfected forever those who are being sanctified."*
*- Hebrews 10:14*

*Psychology Today* describes perfectionism as *"a trait that makes life an endless report card on accomplishments or looks. A fast and enduring track to unhappiness, it is often accompanied by depression and eating disorders. What makes perfectionism so toxic is that while those in its grip desire success, they are most focused on avoiding failure, so theirs is a negative orientation."*

**There are four types of perfectionism that I have experienced:**

- **Perfectionism toward ourselves** resulting from a deeply rooted fear of looking like a failure
- **Perfectionism toward others** that creates hurt in relationships
- **Societal expectation perfectionism** resulting from the media, advertisements, social media, and other forms of peer pressure
- **Christian commitment perfectionism** resulting from legalism, a task-master-God-concept, and an inability to understand Christian growth as a process

All of us battle perfectionistic tendencies to some degree. Regardless of how much you battle perfectionism, you will find these five powerful keys helpful to your freedom from perfectionistic tendencies.

1. **Focus on improvement, not what people think of you**
   – Perfectionists tend to overemphasize people's perceptions of

their looks, possessions, intelligence, etc. Hebrews 10:14 tells us Christians have been perfected but also are being sanctified. When we receive Christ as Savior, we become spiritually perfect in Him. We are perfect in righteousness, protection, soundness of mind, and in every other way. Sanctification is the divinely-empowered process of getting into our experience who we already are in Christ. Healthy people focus on improvement instead of trying to present a perfect image to others.

2. **Do something and celebrate progress** – Those with a religious mindset of performing for the approval of God and others can only be joyful and celebrate when they achieve perfection. This hinders them from attempting new things. The Apostle Paul had a different attitude about this. "Not that I have already attained, or am already perfected; but I press on, that I may lay hold of that for which Christ Jesus has also laid hold of me (Philippians 3:12).

3. **Recognize those who succeed most also seem to fail most** – When toddlers are learning to walk, they "fail" greatly before they walk well. Some might think they do not have the gift of walking because of how difficult it is for them. Rarely does anyone become immediately successful in life's various components. Those who understand the process of growth will not let struggles stop them.

4. **Redefine success** – Success is not a goal to be attained but a state of being. God moves us forward and upward in influence by leading us to become inwardly successful when we don't look successful on the outside. This is true soul prosperity. "Beloved, I pray that you may prosper in all things and be in health, just as your soul prospers" (3 John 2).

5. **Embrace authenticity** – When we open up to others about our struggles, we open the door for grace in and around us. James 4:6 says, "But He gives more grace. Therefore He says, 'God resists the proud, but gives grace to the humble.'" This is especially important for leaders, parents, and teachers. If we are not authentic and demonstrate an unwaveringly successful persona, we withhold

the whole story of our process and potentially enable crippling perfectionistic attitudes in those we lead, parent, and teach.

As we overcome perfectionism, we will increase in joy, hope, skills, and influence.

Declarations:

1. I celebrate progress, not perfection
2. God is making me successful on the inside when I don't seem successful on the outside
3. My authenticity destroys perfectionism in the lives of others

# Overcoming Disappointment

*"Where there is no vision, the people perish..."*

*- Proverbs 29:18*

There are two ways to live. We can live a hopeless life and never be disappointed, or we can live a hope-filled life and experience occasional disappointment. **Hope is the belief that the future will be better than the present, and I have the power to help make it so.** Hope is the confident, joy-filled expectancy that good is coming. Hope is an overall optimistic attitude about the future based on the goodness and promises of God. Yes, it is risky to be a person of hope, but without hope, things begin to die in us and around us. "Where there is no vision (hope), the people perish..." (Proverbs 29:18).

**"Take up the sword of the Spirit, which is the word of God" (Ephesians 6:17)**. It is called a sword because we are supposed to kill something with it: the mindsets in us that oppose God's promises.

Victorious people recognize disappointment is one of our main enemies to be defeated. We each must face five key areas of disappointment:

- **Disappointment with God** – The Psalms are filled with examples of sadness and frustration with what God was seemingly doing or not doing. Bill Johnson, Senior Leader at Bethel Church, says to read the Psalms until you find your voice (or your situation). The Psalms are a strong remedy for being disappointed with God.

- **Disappointment with Yourself** – Who hasn't been angry with themselves about things they did or should have done? The devil is called the Accuser of the Brethren. One of his main tactics to disempower us is to cause us to focus on our weaknesses and faults more than on the strengths we have in Christ. When we are told to "resist the devil" (James 4:7), we are being told, amongst other things, to resist partnering with chronic disappointment with ourselves.

- **Disappointment with Leadership** – Whether it is a governmental leader, church leader, parent, a boss, or some other authority figure, each of us has been hurt in some way by someone over us. Being regularly disappointed and frustrated with our leaders is an attitude we cannot keep if we are going to fulfill our destiny. When you are tempted to criticize a leader, immediately start praying for them. It will accelerate positive solutions and overcome your own negative responses.

- **Disappointment with Those You Lead** – I remember early on in pastoring how I would be frustrated with the people I was leading. I would lower my beliefs about them in proportion to my disappointment in them. The Lord said, "Steve, do you know what your people's biggest problem is? It's you! They are trying to rise above the negative beliefs you have about them and are having difficulty doing so." I began to recognize overcoming disappointment in people was a quality of great leadership.

- **Disappointment with Life in General** – Isaiah 61:1 says, "The anointing heals the broken-hearted." We all experience disappointment that can lead to brokenness in our hearts. Obviously, some have much greater negative circumstances than others, but God promises to heal us.

Biblical heroes like Gideon overcame disappointment, and so will we. God did not just fix the pain in Gideon's heart, but He gave him identity and purpose which brought wholeness and fulfilment. By practicing the above shifts in perspective, I believe that you, too, will be well on your way toward overcoming disappointment and living a hope-filled life.

Declarations:

1. God has healed my heart from disappointments, and He uses me to heal the hearts of others as well
2. The future will be better than the present, and I have the power to help make it happen
3. I courageously walk in biblical optimism, and I release transformational hope wherever I go

# From Victimhood to Victory

*"...seek those things which are above..."*

*- Colossians 3:1*

We are not to be conformed to the thinking of this world (Romans 12:2), but we are to pursue higher thoughts about God, ourselves, others, and our circumstances. As believers, we are to set the tone based on Heaven's truth and perspective, not that of our feelings or popular opinion. When we understand we cannot trust any thought or conclusion that does not have hope attached to it, we are ready for elevated thinking and the transformation it brings.

James 1:2-12 gives great insight into how to change our thought lives from fixating on problems to focusing on advancing the kingdom. Here are four higher spiritual realities revealed in these verses:

1) **A Higher Perspective** – "My brethren, count it all joy when you fall into various trials, knowing that the testing of your faith produces patience. But let patience have its perfect work, that you may be perfect and complete, lacking nothing" (James 1:2-4). Our response to something is almost always more important than the something. When we choose to rejoice in the Lord, incredible forward movement in our lives begins.

2) **A Higher Strategy** – "If any of you lacks wisdom, let him ask of God, who gives to all liberally and without reproach, and it will be given to him. But let him ask in faith, with no doubting, for

he who doubts is like a wave of the sea driven and tossed by the wind. For let not that man suppose that he will receive anything from the Lord; he is a double-minded man, unstable in all his ways" (James 1:5-8). There is always a solution for every situation we face (I Corinthians 10:13). God has supernatural wisdom (strategies, ideas, etc.) for breakthrough in us and around us. As we believe God will give us these higher strategies, He will. Start thanking Him right now for the divine insight being revealed to you.

3) **A Higher Identity** – "Let the lowly brother glory in his exaltation" (James 1:9). Negatively comparing ourselves to others is a lower way of thinking. We may not be as gifted or outwardly blessed as some others, but we are unique and have greatness in us. In Christ, we are a new creation. As we think higher about ourselves by believing who God says we are, it propels us to greater influence. In Numbers 13, the ten spies believed they were like grasshoppers in their own sight. Their interpretation of themselves created their beliefs about the world around them. If we don't embrace our higher identity, then we will perceive ourselves as victims who are powerless to bring change.

4) **A Higher Purpose** – "Blessed is the man who endures temptation; for when he has been approved, he will receive the crown of life which the Lord has promised to those who love Him" (James 1:12). A crown of life indicates authority has been given us. Whatever area we have overcome in our lives is an area where we have authority to bring life to others. Most people's greatest anointing comes from something they battled; therefore, your current struggle is not just about you, but it is about the people you will influence as you overcome. Your purpose in life is not just to fix yourself, but to be a life-releaser and a great influencer.

God loves to take people from crisis to radical influence. These four higher realities will help you get there.

Declarations:

1. I am a person who increasingly walks in higher perspectives, higher strategies, higher identity, and higher purpose
2. James chapter one is exploding with grace-filled revelation into my life and supernaturally creating victory for others and me
3. I think as Jesus thinks

# Key Targets for Victorious Declarations

*"Death and life are in the power of the tongue, And those who love it will eat its fruit."*

- Proverbs 18:21

D eclarations are faith statements proclaiming truths higher than what we are experiencing or feeling. "Faith comes by hearing" (Romans 10:17). We declare in order to convince ourselves of these realities, not to convince other people. Declarations are a main way to renew our minds (Romans 12:2) and to disempower negative strongholds (2 Corinthians 10:4-5).

We accelerate our hope ignition by making declarations. Here are four key areas to target:

1) **Declarations Over Past Prayers** (overcoming vain repetition in prayer) – "Be anxious for nothing, but in everything by prayer and supplication, *with thanksgiving*, let your requests be made known to God; and the peace of God, which surpasses all understanding, will guard your hearts and minds through Christ Jesus" (Philippians 4:6-7). The key phrase in this passage is "with thanksgiving." The moment we add thanksgiving to our prayers, we move from begging into faith. Using the words "thank you" concerning past prayers creates some of the strongest declarations. "Thank you, Father, for touching the hearts of my family with your love." "Thank you for meeting all my financial needs." "Thank you that miracles are increasing for me and through me."

2) **Declarations Over Tomorrow** (overcoming pessimism and passivity about the future) – There are three ways to approach the future. First, we can have foreboding, which is the confident expectation bad is coming. Second, we can be passive, where we neither have a negative nor a positive expectation. Third, we can have faith that good things will happen because of God's promises, God's goodness, and because of what we have prayed in the past. This third approach is catalytic to our beliefs and ultimately our experience. "Tomorrow will be a tremendous day. Every meeting I have will be kingdom-advancing. My family interactions will be blessed. I will move forward in my life in significant ways, and I will release life-changing encounters with God wherever I go."

3) **Declarations Of Our True Identity** (overcoming getting our beliefs from our past experience) – We cannot consistently do what we don't believe we are. For instance, if we try to act like we are righteous while still believing we are sinners, we will not have long lasting success. Gideon had to hear he was a mighty warrior before it started to manifest in him (Judges 6). We, too, need to hear who we really are. Declarations are the main way to do this. "I am righteous, anointed, loving, joy-filled, wise, prosperous, protected, evangelistic, and blessed."

4) **Declarations About the People In Our Lives** (overcoming a lack of hope about others) – Just as we are not who our past says we are, neither are the people in our lives. Certainly, we don't discount the past when it comes to how much access a person will have to me or to the people I love, but highly influential people actually believe in others even more than they believe in themselves. Declarations are a powerful way to upgrade our beliefs about those in our lives. "Susie is a strong lover of people. She is a revivalist who makes great decisions. She is the righteousness of Christ, and she is a person of increasing protection and blessing."

Declarations changed my life. Much of what I am experiencing now is because of what I declared twenty-five years ago when it seemed ridiculous. Why not do an experiment and make at least 100 declarations a day and see what happens?

Declarations:

1. Because life is in the power of the tongue (Proverbs 18:21), I consistently speak life over others, my circumstances, and myself
2. My declarations about my past prayers increase my faith about those things
3. I am who God says I am, not what my past experience says I am

# Kingdom Mindsets for Powerful Beliefs

*"...be transformed by the renewing of your mind..."*
                                                    *- Romans 12:2*

True change and transformation do not come from surrendering and sacrificing our behaviors but our beliefs. Romans 12:2 says, "Be transformed by the renewing of your mind."

We have the power to change what we believe: Abraham, Gideon, Peter, Moses, and many other biblical figures chose to do just that. Each of them overcame defeatist mindsets in the midst of seemingly hopeless circumstances. We are empowered by God to do the same.

Here are five powerful beliefs to renew our minds with that will bring positive transformation in our lives:

1. **Believe God's overall promises for you** – "Let us hold fast the confession of *our* hope without wavering, for He who promised *is* faithful" (Hebrews 10:23). "For all the promises of God in Him *are* Yes, and in Him Amen, to the glory of God through us" (2 Corinthians 1:20). "By which have been given to us exceedingly great and precious promises, that through these you may be partakers of the divine nature" (2 Peter 1:4).

2. **Believe God's specific promises for you** – "Man shall not live by bread alone, but by every word that proceeds from the mouth of God" (Matthew 4:4). All God's promises are true for

us, but the Holy Spirit will breathe prophetic life on those we are to fight with for a season or even for our whole lives. "Take up the sword of the Spirit which is the Word of God" (Ephesians 6:17). 1 Timothy 1:18 gives even greater insight on this: "This charge I commit to you, son Timothy, according to the prophecies previously made concerning you, that by them you may wage the good warfare."

3. **Believe the spirit realm is more real than the physical realm** – "By faith we understand that the worlds were framed by the word of God, so that the things which are seen were not made of things which are visible" (Hebrews 11:3). "The fool has said in his heart, 'There is no God'" (Psalm 14:1). Logic tells us if something exists now, then something has always existed, and that something is a Someone. As we acknowledge this, then we recognize the importance of the spirit realm.

4. **Believe you are significant with unique giftings and assignments** – "So we, *being* many, are one body in Christ, and individually members of one another. Having then gifts differing according to the grace that is given to us, *let us use them*" (Romans 12:5-6). There is nobody like you. There is no one who can say it like you can say it. You have grace for a special assignment and to influence specific types of people.

5. **Believe this is the year of breakthrough for long-standing issues** – "So Jesus asked his father, 'How long has this been happening to him?' And he said, 'From childhood'" (Mark 9:21). Jesus healed this boy after years of no breakthrough. The Bible frequently mentions the length of time an illness or problem has existed to build faith in us for long-standing problems. When we don't give up, our faith will draw heaven toward us and increase the likelihood of seeing the miracle happen.

Remember, we first believe and then see, not the other way around. If we want to see something different, then we are called to believe something higher than what we are experiencing. These five beliefs are a great place to start and are sure to cause powerful transformation and freedom in your life.

Declarations:

1. I am believing God's promises for my life like never before
2. I am in a season of great breakthrough in my emotions, my relationships, my finances, and my influence
3. I consistently inspire others to walk in great faith, hope, and love

# Do Not Withdraw Your Faith

*"Therefore I say to you, whatever things you ask when you pray, believe that you receive them, and you will have them."*

*- Mark 11:24*

Years ago I sensed the Lord say to me, "Steve, you have a habit of withdrawing your faith after ministry or prayer based on what you feel or see. I am going to help you overcome this because where you are going, you cannot take this tendency with you." We are called to stay in faith, no matter what we see. We are to cultivate belief that it is impossible for nothing to happen when we pray, minister, or implement God's wisdom in our lives.

Here are four reasons not to withdraw your faith:

1.  **Faith believes without seeing** – "Therefore I tell you, whatever you ask for in prayer, believe that you have received it, and it will be yours" (Mark 11:24). God wants us to believe we receive at the time of prayer what we have been praying for. Obviously, these requests need to be consistent with the heart of God, but we are told to believe we have it at the moment we pray. How long should we believe this when we don't see it manifesting? Five minutes? Five days? Five years? Five decades? I believe even longer, if needed. And, as we stay in faith, grace will flow to change anything in us that needs to be changed in order for us to see desires fulfilled.

2. **Seeds take time to grow into a harvest** – "Do not be deceived: God cannot be mocked. A man reaps what he sows...Let us not become weary in doing good, for at the proper time we will reap a harvest if we do not give up" (Galatians 6:7-9). "I planted the seed, Apollos watered it, but God has been making it grow" (I Corinthians 2:6). When farmers don't see an immediate crop after planting seeds, they don't withdraw their faith. In spiritual things, it usually takes time for seeds sown to grow into a harvest.

3. **It is a primary way to overcome the accuser** – "For the accuser of our brothers and sisters, who accuses them before our God day and night, has been hurled down" (Revelation 12:10). The devil not only accuses us before God, but constantly accuses us in our thoughts when we emphasize behavior over identity. As we stay in faith concerning our identity in Christ (our righteousness, our authority, etc.), we "hurl down" the accuser's lies that want to neutralize us.

4. **It is a main way to practice Philippians 4:6-8** – "Do not be anxious about anything, but in every situation, by prayer and petition, with thanksgiving, present your requests to God. And the peace of God, which transcends all understanding, will guard your hearts and your minds in Christ Jesus. Finally, brothers and sisters, whatever is true...think about such things" (Philippians 4:6-8). This is a roadmap to peace and spiritual confidence. The phrase "with thanksgiving" is the key to stay in faith. Once we move into thanksgiving in prayer, we move from begging into belief. Verse eight reveals to us that we can actually think on purpose, thus overcoming the tendency to withdraw our faith.

We are people who stay in faith and hope. A great place to practice this is to intentionally thank God for His unseen work in our past prayers as well as those which have been answered. We can start with these smaller areas, and then move onto our bigger concerns. Something always happens when we pray in faith from a thankful heart.

Declarations:

1. I live by faith, not by sight
2. After I minister, pray, or obey God, I stay in faith, and even increase my faith, concerning what I did
3. I regularly water my past actions and prayers with thanksgiving

# Great Confidence in Hope Part 1

*"Now this is the confidence that we have in him, that if we ask anything according to His will, He hears us."*

*- 1 John 5:14*

God has called us to walk in spiritual confidence. Even so, at times we all have situations where we don't feel as confident as we'd like. Here are four keys for you to increase your confidence in Him:

1) **Get your identity from God, not your past**

   If we don't know who God says we are, we risk putting our confidence in our own ability. If we get our identity from our past, we will be plagued by doubt and inner weakness. God does not define us by our worst day, the worst thing that has happened to us, or our worst mistake. Corrie ten Boom put it well when she said, "God has taken our sin. He has thrown it into the sea of forgetfulness, and He has posted a sign that says, 'No fishing allowed'" (Micah 7:19). We are not who our past says we are, we are who God says we are—no longer slaves, but children and heirs! (Galatians 4:7).

2) **Realize everyone battles some level of insecurity**

   Have you ever thought about the fact that God does not hide the insecurities of those He used in the Bible? He doesn't just play us the 'highlight' reel, but He delights in every part of each person's story and journey with Him. Every great person has battled, or is battling, some level of inner doubt about who they are and what they can do. How encouraging it is to know we are not alone, even though it may often feel like we are the only one dealing with insecurity. The enemy uses comparison to shift our focus to what we lack; imagine how differently our outlook and response to situations would be if we took those opportunities as a challenge to discover and declare who and what we actually are!

## 3) Understand perfect love casts out all fear

1 John 4:18 reveals that God's love is the antidote to fear and insecurity. This is a twofold process: first, as we experience God's love in our own life, we naturally become more confident. Secondly, as we focus on whole-heartedly loving and meeting the needs of those around us, we will be less prone to shrink back in introspection, comparison, shame, and self-criticism. Instead, perfect love helps us grow in self-awareness and step into a lifestyle marked with confidence and intentionality that adds value to our relationships.

## 4) Deal with legitimate guilt in your life

We are people who love God and sincerely want to please Him. It is important, though, to keep in mind that many lack confidence because they haven't dealt with underlying sin or learned how to tune out the devil's accusations about things Jesus has already covered. Do we, at times, need to walk out the consequences of poor choices, or address bad fruit that we have allowed to develop in our lives? Will we need to repent of actions and seek forgiveness of others? Of course. Does that mean we need to isolate ourselves out of guilt and shame? Definitely not! As we meditate on and declare the truth of our forgiveness and new identity in Christ, we will defeat the great enemies of guilt and condemnation.

These four keys will help you walk in this confidence like never before. The next devotional will give you three more powerful keys.

Declarations:

1. I am a confident, hope-filled person whose influence is increasing dramatically

2. God is supernaturally causing me to overcome guilt and condemnation, and I have an unusual gift to help others do so as well
3. God's perfect love is casting out fear in others and in me

# Great Confidence in Hope Part 2

*"Now this is the confidence that we have in him, that if we ask anything according to His will, He hears us."*

*- 1 John 5:14*

The previous devotional listed four keys for you to increase your confidence in God. We continue here with three more keys to help you grow in spiritual confidence.

### 5) Be filled with the Holy Spirit – He gives confidence!

"And when they had prayed, the place where they were assembled together was shaken; and they were all filled with the Holy Spirit, and they spoke the word of God with boldness" (Acts 4:31). Consider Peter, an unstable fisherman, who denied Christ three times who was then baptized and filled with the Holy Spirit in the book of Acts. It was after this powerful experience that he became one of the most bold, confident people who has ever walked on the planet! The Holy Spirit supernaturally empowers us and causes us to become who we were created to be in all its fullness. As we pursue deeper encounters in the Spirit and believe for fresh fillings, we too will walk in greater confidence—living a vibrant life with hope, boldness and purpose!

### 6) Understand your assignment

Negative comparison to others greatly hinders our spiritual confidence. No one else will ever be a better you than you. Do you want to know what the great news about that is? It means we aren't called to be like everyone else! The gifts that you carry, the way that you think, how you communicate, your personality—they're all purposefully created and endorsed by God in fulfilling unique assignments only you can carry out in touching people's lives and reaching hearts. Ask God for wisdom and clarity on this (James 1:5), and to discover what your unique assignment is: for this week, for this season, and for your life. Once we have clarity about what our assignment is and what it isn't, confidence will naturally follow because we will be doing what we're supposed to be doing—living in the heart of God's will.

### 7) Believe your past prayers are working!

"Now this is the confidence that we have in him, that if we ask anything according to His will, He hears us. And if we know that He hears us, whatever we ask, we know that we have the petitions that we have asked of Him" (1 John 5:14-15). If we actually believe that our prayers are working, we will have greater confidence. It is impossible for us to pray and have nothing happen; God is always working on our behalf, whether it is overtly or seemingly behind the scenes. He is continually narrating God stories in our lives, weaving His faithfulness, covering, and love into a tapestry of splendor. When we look at circumstances through the lens of our past prayers, then we will have confidence that God is moving powerfully in the uncertainties we face.

You are entering a new season of confidence. God is touching you, healing you of insecurities, and releasing boldness over you for the days ahead. You are important in what he is doing around the world!

Declarations:

1. I am filled with the confidence of the Holy Spirit in all things
2. I am gloriously unique, and my assignments are essential for worldwide transformation
3. God is always working on my behalf in perfect timing, weaving all my days and all my prayers into an exceptionally beautiful story

# How to Have a Joy-Filled Day

*"For I know the thoughts that I think toward you, says the LORD,*
*thoughts of peace and not of evil, to give you a future and a hope."*
*- Jeremiah 29:11*

E ach day brings tasks and to-do lists, meetings to attend, assignments to fulfill, secret place times with the Lord to be prioritized, and all the interactions that keep life moving ahead. Some may seem inevitable, but how we think and talk about them isn't. In fact, our mindsets and words about these daily moments dramatically impact the quality of our experience and our capacity to bring our best to every situation.

We can choose one of three ways to approach each line item on the calendar:

1) **With Foreboding and Worry** – Hope is the confident, joyful expectation that good is coming. Foreboding is an expectation that bad is coming. Worry is imagining life without God, rehearsing a future without expecting God's promises to manifest themselves in powerful ways.

   Just as governments can seed clouds to bring about rain, I used to seed the clouds of my future with pessimism. I would think and say things that reflected inferior beliefs. For instance, if I had a meeting with a challenging person, I would release dread into the spiritual clouds concerning that meeting. This lack of victorious thinking hindered how much God could do.

The truth is, God is always bigger than any circumstance. He always turns up and continually looks to establish His grace and power in every context. When we align our beliefs with this powerful reality, it not only enables us to partner with His higher perspectives but also makes a way for us to influence and empower those around us to do the same.

2) **With Passivity** – When we are passive, we have a "whatever will be, will be" attitude. Passivity makes us emotionally neutral to an event, meeting, or to a new day. We don't have any big expectations in the positive or negative. We believe faithfulness is simply showing up.

When we allow ourselves to passively approach our days ahead, it's not long before we find ourselves established in a cycle of allowing life to "happen to us," rather than positioning ourselves in a way where we "happen to life." We are God's empowered people. He wants us engaged and proactive in everything we do. Having high expectations isn't simply wishful thinking, it's taking dominion over every circumstance, taking ground where the Lord has given us influence, and joining our "Yes" with heaven's to see His kingdom established in mighty ways.

3) **With Hope and Faith** – This is the highest level of preparation and approach to engaging with what is in front of us. Just as I mentioned earlier, hope is the confident, joyful expectation that good is coming. Faith believes something is happening in the positive, even when it is not seen. Those who function in these mindsets understand that faithfulness is not a matter of simply showing up, but how we think before we show up and when we get there. Faith thinkers seed the clouds of their future through positive thoughts and declarations like, "Tomorrow is going to be a great day," or "This meeting is going to change the world."

Expectation is another word for faith. When Jesus said in Matthew 9:29, "According to your faith, let it be to you," it could be translated, "According to your expectation, let it be to you." I don't want to be in the habit of expecting negative things to happen, or even nothing at all; I want to stir up the expectation that great things will occur in the days ahead. Diligently establishing this as our automatic approach to life will build inner victory in us, and will bring increasing breakthrough to those around us.

Let's go for it and see how powerfully hope, faith, and expectancy can transform our minds, hearts, and circumstances.

Declarations:

1. I have great hope for the future because I believe God's promises
2. I attach faith to the specific things I will do today and to the things I will do in the future
3. I am boldly overcoming foreboding and passivity, and I cause multitudes to do the same

# 3 Things Not to Do When Feeling Like a Failure

*"Yet in all these things we are more than conquerors through Him who loved us."*

*- Romans 8:37*

The feeling of failure can be paralyzing. Whether we're experiencing a setback or we seem to fall short of society's standard of success, there are moments and even seasons in life where we battle discouragement about who we are and how we are doing. Our emotional response to this can range from mild discouragement to full-blown depression. What should we do in these times?

There certainly are many positive things *to do*, but I am going to share three things *not to do* when you feel like a failure:

1. **Don't Make Failure Your Identity** – You may have experienced a failing, but you are not a failure. We don't deny our experience, but we cannot get our identity from it. One of the greatest keys to victory is to maintain a solid belief in who God says you are no matter what your experience says. Certainly, cultivating healthy beliefs about ourselves is not the only thing we do to live triumphantly, but it is the most important thing. "Let the weak say 'I am strong'" (Joel 3:10). Keep saying you are a success, even when you feel like a failure.

2. **Don't Quit** – Winston Churchill was asked to speak at a graduation commencement after World War II. He stood up and

said, "Never give up. Never give up. Never give up." Then he sat down. His life was the message. This is a speech we all need to hear over and over again. Another powerful phrase to remember is: "Never stop starting." Every day start again with the behaviors, plans, and attitudes you want to have. "And let us not grow weary while doing good, for in due season we shall reap if we do not lose heart" (Galatians 6:9). We will reap a good harvest "if we do not lose heart." Wow, what a promise! Let's not quit.

3. **Don't Become Lazy** – When we seem to fail, there is a tendency to want to hide and withdraw. Yes, we will at times need to rest and be alone to regroup and recharge, but we cannot withdraw and escape every time we're disappointed. No matter where you are in life, there is a step forward available to you. As you move ahead in that one thing, more light will be given to see where to go from there. Remember, your response to something is almost always more important than the something. As we maintain our commitments in discouraging times, we will build a victorious-living "muscle" that will increase our load bearing capacity for the days ahead.

You are NOT a failure. You are "more than a conqueror " (Romans 8:37). There is grace on you today to shake off the feelings of failure. You are called to encourage others who are battling the same. It is indeed a new day of increased hope and victory for you and those in your life.

Declarations:

1. I never give up. I never give up. I never give up
2. I am not a failure, but I am strong, victorious, an overcomer, resilient, adaptable, and I find solutions for every challenge I face
3. Even when I am discouraged, I have an unusual and supernatural ability to remain faithful to my commitments

# 5 Steps To Radical Mind Renewal

*"...be transformed by the renewing of your mind..."*

*- Rom 12:2*

This powerful verse has changed Wendy's and my life, and has since become the pillar of our ministry, Igniting Hope. We have seen that renewing our minds with God's truth transforms us, manifesting tangible hope in our lives.

Here are some great truths we can glean from Romans 12:2:

- Whatever we renew our minds with creates our future experience
- The past cannot block our future transformation, but the beliefs we rehearse can
- All limits are removed from our lives! Because there is no limit to how much we can renew our minds with truth, there is no limit to how much we can be transformed

Biblical mind renewal is the decision to rehearse thoughts based on the promises of God, rather than rehearsing conclusions based on our feelings or experiences. This doesn't mean we should deny the existence of negative circumstances when they occur, but we don't allow them to dictate our beliefs and hope levels for the future.

To help you on this journey, here are the five steps we have learned that bring transformational mind renewal:

1. **Identify areas of your life that are not "glistening with hope"** – "Now may the God of hope fill you...in believing..." (Romans 15:13). Our hope level is the indicator of whether we're believing lies or truth. A lack of hope is the "check engine" light that lets us know we are believing lies. You may, for example, realize that you do not have much hope for your future potential. This becomes an area to target in Step 2.

2. **Verbalize the lie fueling this lack of hope** – As we do this, we bring these problem-causing beliefs into the light and start the process of disempowering them. For instance, if you struggle with hope for your future, you may identify that you believe the lie that "I am who my past says I am, rather than who God says I am." After recognizing and speaking this aloud, you will be able to see clearly that you're believing a lie that opposes the truth.

3. **Laugh at the lie and release it** – "A merry heart does good, *like* medicine..." (Proverbs 17:22). Laughter, an important aspect of joy, is one of the main ways we stay emotionally and physically healthy. To laugh, we need to let go of something. We cannot hold on to pessimism, offense, frustration, victim mindsets, or unworthiness and laugh at the same time.

4. **Identify the truth** – "...the truth will make you free." (John 8:32). We first get free in our emotions, then in our circumstances. Ask this question: "What do I need to believe in order to have hope in this area?" A key shift happens when you discover the truth needed to displace the lie.

5. **Rehearse this truth in thoughts and speech** – We don't make a path through a forest by walking through it once. This is also true as we develop new mindsets. As we begin to think and regularly declare God's truth in an area, greater levels of freedom rise up inside of us and begin to manifest in our experience. By practicing these steps, you will walk in renewed hope and freedom that will transform your life and those around you.

One of the greatest revelations we can have is that we can choose what we will believe. These five steps will help you believe freedom-causing truth and see transformation in your emotions and circumstances like never before.

Declarations:

1. I renew my mind with truth, not lies
2. I see life through the hope-filled lens of God's promises, my biblical identity, and the prayers I have prayed in the past—I am very intentional and strategic in how I renew my mind
3. I have an extraordinary ability to help others renew their mind with truth.

# 5 Lies About World Events

*"Let us hold fast the confession of our hope without wavering, for He who promised is faithful."*

*- Hebrews 10:23*

In I Kings 19, Elijah flees to a cave, despite having just come through one of the greatest victories of his life. He felt tired, disappointed, and spiritually depleted and, in his weakened state, believed he was all alone. God's response gave him a perspective upgrade: there were 7,000 others who had not "bowed the knee to Baal" (I Kings 19:18). In other words, there was 7,000 times more happening on his behalf than Elijah thought. I believe, even today, God is doing 7,000 times more in the situations we're facing than we think He is.

Most spiritual heaviness, discouragement, and depression come from believing lies, not from our circumstances or physical ailments. As we replace lies with truth, we will increase in both hope and influence.

Here are five lies to conquer about world events:

1. **I am a victim of what is happening around the world** – A victim mindset believes we are powerless to bring change unless circumstances around us change first. Those with this belief system will be greatly hindered in forward movement and influence. The promises of God obliterate victim thinking. "Let us hold fast the confession of our hope without wavering, for He who promised is faithful" (Hebrews 10:23).

2. **There is no hope for our future** – There is always hope. "Now may the God of hope fill you with all joy and peace in believing, that you may abound in hope by the power of the Holy Spirit" (Romans 15:13). My wife, Wendy, once asked the Lord, "Aren't some circumstances hopeless?" In response, she heard, "Wendy, I will give you permission to be hopeless about anything I am hopeless about." Truly, there are no hopeless circumstances, only people without hope. Once people get true hope, it is impossible for circumstances to stay the same.

3. **I should disengage from society and just wait for Jesus to return** – Christians often lack hope for the future when they embrace a defeatist "end times" view. This expectation contradicts the truth of what we should believe and pray, "Your kingdom come, your will be done, on earth as it is in heaven" (Matthew 6:10). We are not called to withdraw, but to believe our prayers are working and that we are to "do business until (He) comes" (Luke 19:13).

4. **The devil is winning** – We may believe the devil is winning if we feed on the negative reports rather than testimonies of what God is doing around the world. It may feel true that darkness is gaining ground, but we are called to instead believe these powerful words of Jesus, "I will build my church and the gates of hell will not prevail" (Matthew 16:18).

5. **I cannot thrive in these circumstances** – Paul said, "I can do all things through Christ who strengthens me" (Philippians 4:13). In verses 11-12, Paul declares his contentment despite circumstances. In other words, he is supernaturally empowered by God to be inwardly successful, come what may. He says he will thrive in every situation, and so will we. Once we hear and believe truth, we receive supernatural hope and radical breakthrough— anything is possible to him who believes.

Let's learn from Elijah and carry our victories with us. As we do, we defeat the lies that threaten to take us out. Discouragement and hopelessness are not our portion: God is working all things for our good, and He's stacked the deck in our favor.

Declarations:

1. God is doing 7,000 times more than I think He is doing
2. I feed on the Bible, its promises, and testimonies far more than I feed on what the media is saying
3. I dramatically influence world events through my prayers, obedience, declarations, my love, and my hope

# "I'm Winning Too"

*"Beloved, I pray that you may prosper in all things and be in health, just as your soul prospers."*

*- 3 John 2*

When my grandson, Caden, was about three years old, he and our family were in a park in Redding. As we were getting ready to leave, Caden was very slow in getting from the park trail to the car. To get him moving, I decided to pull out some of my high-level motivational skills and said:

"Caden, let's race!"

He did not move at all. I knew I needed to take my words to a greater level, so I said:

"Caden, I'm winning!"

Still no movement. Without skipping a beat, Caden said:

"I'm winning too!"

"Wow," I thought. "Caden is in last place, and he thinks he is a winner. He has some strong beliefs!"

Caden thought he was a winner because he was not in the same race as his grandpa. He was winning the "race" of what three-year-olds do—looking at rocks, leaves, and birds.

Many misdiagnose themselves as failures because they don't know what race they're in. If we think we are in the race to be the most popular, to be the most beautiful, to have the most money, or to be the most successful, then we will almost certainly believe we are losing at life in some way.

**One of God's main pathways toward strength in leadership and influence is for us to develop inner success before we look successful on the outside.** God highlighted this to me in the early '90s while I was pastoring in Central Nevada. At that time, I thought it was an inconvenient season to develop this inner success. Many aspects of my life at the time were telling me I was not "winning too," but a failure:

I had an unsuccessful car.

My salary was not successful.

My hair was starting to be unsuccessful (haha!).

My church size was not successful.

Our home, an older single-wide trailer, was not successful.

I heard, "Now is the time to believe you are a winner and start winning in your emotions like never before." As my wife Wendy says, emotions don't validate truth; they just validate what I believe to be true. It was a season of learning to prosper in my soul. "Beloved, I pray that you may prosper in all things and be in health, just as your soul prospers" (3 John 2). Soul prosperity is the biblical wording for this inward victory. We are told our physical health and our prosperity in all outward things result from us prospering in our souls. What an incredible promise and direction for our lives!

Here are three ways to prosper in your soul:

1. **Identify the season you are in** – What is happening in us is more important than what is happening through us. As we can put language to what God is doing in us, we will know what race we're in

2. **Celebrate progress, not perfection** – The religious and perfectionistic mindset only celebrates and becomes joyful with perfection, but families celebrate progress

3. **Reject worldly standards for success** – Success is not a goal to be attained but a state of being. While we know God desires to bless us in every way, we are to reject seeking success instead of Him as well as the temptation to get our identity from these blessings

Caden said, "I'm winning too!" Why don't you say that right now? They are life-changing words that will ignite hope in your present circumstances and future vision.

Declarations:

1. I am becoming increasingly successful on the inside, even when I don't seem successful on the outside
2. I understand the season I am in, and I understand the most important things God is doing in me during this time
3. I am relentless. There is no stopping me as I move from inner victory to transformation in my circumstances

# Feelings Don't Validate Truth, They Validate What We Believe

*"For the weapons of our warfare are not carnal but mighty in God for pulling down strongholds…"*

*- 2 Corinthians 10:4*

The two main sources of disempowering beliefs in our lives are past experiences and feelings. We don't deny our past or our feelings, but we cannot get our beliefs from them. They are the arguments and high things of 2 Corinthians 10:5 that will create negative strongholds in our lives if we don't bring them into captivity to the victory and identity we have in Christ.

"Casting down arguments and every high thing that exalts itself against the knowledge of God, bringing every thought into captivity to the obedience of Christ" (2 Corinthians 10:4-5).

When I was born again as a 19-year-old, I would only believe I was saved when I felt saved. If I went to church on Sunday feeling discouraged or weighed down by temptation or doubt, I would respond to another altar call and get saved again, just to make sure.

This went on for a while until the Lord spoke to my heart saying, "I have good news for you. You are saved even when you don't feel saved." I thought, "That is amazing! I thought feelings were the highest indicator of truth there was."

Even after hearing this, I would still want to respond to salvation altar calls when I didn't feel saved, but I heard this: "Steve, do not go down there. Stay in your seat. When you believe you are saved, you will start feeling saved." **Good feelings follow good beliefs.**

In my wife Wendy's book, *Victorious Emotions*, she says feelings don't validate truth, they just validate what we believe to be true. This is an important insight for us. If we want a different emotion, we will need a different belief. "Now may the God of hope fill you with all joy and peace **in believing**" (Romans 15:13). The emotions of hope, joy, and peace increase as we believe the truth instead of lies.

**My decision to believe I was saved when I did not feel saved was greater spiritual warfare than if I had rebuked the devil for 30 minutes.** It was high-level warfare.

We also activate this stronghold-demolishing warfare when:

- We believe we are strong when we feel weak
- We believe we are righteous when we feel unworthy
- We believe we are anointed when we don't feel anointed
- We believe we are influential when we feel powerless
- We believe we courageous when we feel paralyzed by fear
- We believe we are healed when our condition seems unchanged
- We believe our actions are significant when they feel insignificant

**Transformation happens when we renew our minds with truths higher than what we are feeling and experiencing.** We don't deny the facts of our experience, but we believe in truths higher than the facts. Certainly, focusing on our beliefs is not the only thing we do to see breakthrough and increase, but it is one of the most important priorities we can have.

As we push against this emotional resistance with the truth about our identity and truth from God's promises, we will develop the belief muscles necessary to walk in hope-filled victory and increase our load-bearing capacity.

Declarations:

1. My beliefs are rooted in faith, not my feelings
2. I am righteous, powerful, and anointed even when I don't feel like it
3. I am a radical breaker of strongholds with every truth I decide to believe

# Five Excuses of a Victim Mindset

*"I can do all things through Christ who strengthens me."*
                                                    *- Philippians 4:13*

"I was afraid, and I went and hid your talent in the ground" (Matthew 25:25). So said the person in the Parable of the Talents who received the one talent. He did not increase what he had like the other two in the parable because he had excuses. When he didn't meet the master's stewardship expectations, he declared himself a victim of an unfair system and his own emotions. He certainly is not the character in this story that we want to emulate.

The victim mindset is one of the biggest lies for the New Covenant believer to defeat. It has neutralized many from getting free in their emotions and circumstances. Recognizing common excuses can help us avoid the pitfalls of the one-talent servant. Here are five beliefs that fuel the victim mindset:

- **I Don't Have Enough Time** – We have more time available to us than we might think. If our doctor told us we must be still for two hours a day or we will die, we would find time to be still for two hours a day. The issue is not so much a lack of time but a lack of desire for change, or a lack of awareness of how bad beliefs about our time frustrate fruitfulness.

- **I Don't Have Enough Money** – A perceived lack of money neutralizes many, but these two truths will help defeat this excuse.

1) "Decide and He will provide," and 2) "Provision follows quality decisions." Something powerful happens when we make a quality decision. "Seek first the kingdom and all these things will be added to you" (Matthew 6:33). As we believe and move forward, we realize we already have the resources we need to start the flow of greater provision. This is illustrated by the seemingly impoverished widow in 2 Kings 4 who supernaturally discovered she already had the source for abundant provision.

- **I Will Probably Fail** – On one level, this is probably true because those who succeed most also seem to fail most. It is rare for anyone to start a new habit or new assignment and not struggle to do it well at first.

- **I Don't Have the Proper Skills** – When Wendy and I first considered writing a book, we thought, "But we have never written a book before." That's where every author begins! We each can start small toward learning skills that advance us in our destiny. There has never been a time in human history where we are more set up to acquire the expertise needed to make our dreams a reality.

- **People Are Holding Me Back** – Despite our feelings, we are not victims to other people's actions or influence over us. David had a dad who did not believe in him, brothers who belittled him, and a king who tried to kill him, but he still fulfilled his calling. Joseph fulfilled his dream and destiny even though his brothers sold him into slavery, Potiphar's wife falsely accused him of rape, and the chief butler forgot him. Daniel lived in an extremely ungodly culture but still overcame and fulfilled his assignment for decades. These Old Testament heroes overcame difficult people and so can we.

One of the best definitions for repentance is to change the way you think. As we start the process of repenting of these excuses by recognizing them, renouncing them, and replacing them with truth, we will find God's grace helping us to live powerfully as victors, not victims.

Declarations:

1. I am a victor, not a victim
2. I already have what I need to thrive in life and influence
3. I am incredibly gifted to free people from the victim mindset

# The Lid is Off

*"...all things are possible to him who believes."*

- *Mark 9:23*

I f you put fleas in a jar and place a lid on the jar, the fleas will learn to jump to the top just enough to avoid hitting the lid. You can then remove the lid and the fleas will not jump out even with the lid gone.

How can we get past the supposed lids on our lives?

1. **Realize the lid is already off** – "All things *are* possible to him who believes" (Mark 9:23).

2. **Don't get your beliefs from the past** – We don't deny the past, we just cannot get our beliefs from it. In 2 Corinthians 10:4-5, we are called to pull down strongholds and demolish arguments that are exalting themselves above the knowledge of God. Many of our biggest strongholds are created by regularly agreeing with past experience instead of what God has said.

3. **Step out of the boat** – Peter took a risk and walked on water (Matthew 14:22-33). He found the walking on water lid was off by taking a risk and stepping out of the boat. He was not 100% successful, but he tried. Often, new levels of breakthrough are on the other side of new levels of risk.

4. **Stop speaking self-limiting words** – When God called Jeremiah to be a prophet, he said, "'Ah, Lord God! Behold, I do not know how to speak, for I am only a youth.' But the Lord said to me, 'Do not say, 'I am only a youth'" (Jeremiah 1:6-7). Many reinforce imaginary lids because of false humility, an imbalanced desire to be authentic, and undisciplined speech.

5. **Develop a no-limits mindset** – If God wanted us to think small, He did a bad job of letting us know. He instead teaches us in the word that: a) All things are possible to believers (Mark 9:23), b) We will do greater works than Jesus (John 14:12), c) We can do all things (Philippians 4:13), and d) We can move mountains by speaking to them (Mark 11:23).

Roger Bannister was the first person to run a mile in less than four minutes in 1954. The experts had said it was impossible. They said there was a lid that prevented human beings from running that fast, despite training and multiple attempts. Amazingly, within three years of Bannister's feat, ten others did it as well (and now over 1,400 people have run a sub-four-minute mile). When we break through self-imposed mental limitations, we show others that it's possible to do the same.

**Matthew 7:7 greatly contributes to the no-limits lifestyle.**

"Ask, and it will be given to you; seek, and you will find; knock, and it will be opened to you. For everyone who asks receives, and he who seeks finds, and to him who knocks it will be opened."

Hey, flea! The lid is off. You can leave the small container you're in. It's time to go where you never thought you'd go. It's time to do what you never thought you'd do. (Just don't get on my dog, Duncan.)

Declarations:

1. Because I am a supernatural creation in Christ, I am not bound by earthly limitations
2. I am courageous and relentless to do what seems impossible
3. My breakthrough breaks barriers of seeming impossibility for multitudes

# Should I Feel Good About Myself?

*"My grace is sufficient for you, for My strength is made perfect in weakness."*

*- 2 Corinthians 12:9*

I remember having a conversation with a leader who was concerned about his thinking. He was about ready to enter a building project, and he was finding himself fixating on money more than he wanted to. His conclusion about this was that there was something wrong with him.

I told him this was the wrong conclusion to make. Because he was growing in influence and load-bearing capacity, his weaknesses were being exposed. This exposure was not for his condemnation, but simply revealed areas to be strengthened as his influence grows.

It is like a sports team that plays better competition. This stronger opponent will reveal flaws the team was not even aware of, and will often lead to them making the conclusion they are losers. That would be the wrong belief: they have simply moved up to a new league where they haven't yet proven themselves. If the team maintains a belief that they are constantly improving, the players will learn and grow into the new level. If they conclude that they're simply not winners, they could be tempted to quit.

If we only choose to do things we cannot fail at, then we are like the one-talent servant in The Parable of the Talents in Matthew 25. We will let fear, perfectionism, and passivity rob us of our potential. We reduce our lives by playing small.

As we seek to embrace our true identity and purpose, we will have our weaknesses revealed to us in great ways. We will be tempted to feel bad about ourselves and lose confidence. I believe this is a big problem. Small thinking and limiting beliefs about ourselves will block us from what we were created to do. Some would object to this thought because they believe people may conclude they are okay when they really are not. Yes, this may happen, but it is important to realize the most transformational doctrinal and identity beliefs have the biggest potential for abuse. We cannot let this fear stop us from moving into what Graham Cooke would describe as brilliant thinking.

If you are a follower of Jesus and you are seeking to go higher in beliefs and influence, here are a few reasons you should feel good about yourself right now:

1. **The joy of the Lord is your strength (Nehemiah 8:10)** – The religious mindset constantly believes we are not measuring up and that God is mad at us. It is impossible to truly embrace joy without feeling good about ourselves.

2. **Delighting in the Lord will give us the desires of our heart (Psalm 37:4)** – Again, it is impossible to delight in the Lord without feeling good about who we are. We will have to let go of striving, condemnation, and perfectionism.

3. **He is strong when we are weak** – "But he said to me (Paul), 'My grace is sufficient for you, for my power is made perfect in weakness.' Therefore I will boast all the more gladly of my weaknesses, so that the power of Christ may rest upon me" (2 Corinthians 12:9). Paul said he would boast all the more gladly in weaknesses (feel good about himself) because he realized every weakness in him was a place where God would reveal His strength.

We do not withhold approval from a toddler who is not walking perfectly, so let's not withhold approval of ourselves while we are learning to walk in higher joy, hope, relationships, life management, etc. As we celebrate ourselves, we will gain strength and momentum for our lives.

Declarations:

1. I am growing incredibly in not only loving myself but liking myself
2. I get excited when my flaws are revealed as I seek to walk higher in beliefs and habits
3. I love the process of growing into my potential

# Hope-Filled Bible Reading

*"Now may the God of hope fill you with all joy and peace in believing,
that you may abound in hope by the power of the Holy Spirit."*
                                                                — *Romans 15:13*

The Word of God is such a tremendous gift to help us see as God sees, to view ourselves, others, circumstances, and all of life from His higher perspective. While there are many opinions, insights, and interpretations of the Bible, I believe one of the most important is to read God's word through the lens of hope.

Here are some of the tools I believe God has given me for reading the Bible from a hope-filled perspective. From this verse we can conclude:

- Increased hope is the evidence we are believing truth
- We cannot trust any conclusion in our life that does not have hope attached to it
- If our Bible reading does not bring hope, we are probably not interpreting it correctly

Here are two verses that are foundational to helping our Bible reading increase our hope levels:

> *"For by one offering He has perfected forever those who are being sanctified," (Hebrews 10:14).*

*"Likewise you also, reckon (consider) yourselves to be dead indeed to sin, but alive to God in Christ Jesus our Lord," (Romans 6:11).*

When we become born again (John 3:3) through believing in Christ's finished work, we immediately become "perfected forever" in all ways (righteousness, forgiveness, power, obedience, health, provision, etc.).

Sanctification is the process of getting into our experience who we already are. The beginning point of this sanctification is to believe (consider, reckon) that we are perfected, but also dead to sin and alive to God, meaning we are:

- Dead to any tendency to sin or do wrong
- Dead to any consequence of sin (curses of any kind)
- Alive to obedience and to doing all the Bible expects in thoughts, actions, and manifest blessing

This creates an exciting adventure of discovery every time we open our Bibles. We get to discover what we are dead to and what we are alive to. When we ask, "What part of sin does this verse tell me I am dead to, and what part of righteousness does it tell me I am alive to?", then our Bible reading becomes increasingly hope-filled. It helps us to break off lies, establish our biblical identity, and continually feast on what Jesus has done for us.

Some might ask, "But won't this lead to more sin because people won't take their negative behavior seriously if they focus on where they are dead to sin and alive in God?" Yes, some may do this, but we cannot let this fear rob us of the power of pursuing hope-filled Bible reading. If you are not sure this is the right direction for you, why don't you try this plan as an experiment for a month and see what happens. I believe the results will be powerful for you.

Declarations:

1. Every time I read the Bible, I discover new aspects of Christ's victory and of my supernatural identity
2. I am a powerful, hope-filled believer
3. I am dead to sin but alive to God in every way

# The Snoopy Anointing

*"Therefore take heed how you hear..."*

*- Luke 8:18*

We used to have a yellow Labrador named Snoopy. He often slept all day in our house, but there was one thing which would jolt him out of a deep slumber: any movement of his leash on our laundry room shelf. Even if the leash was accidentally and only slightly moved, it didn't matter to Snoopy. When he heard this apparent good news, he bounded into the laundry room and often pulled future walks into his present experience. His incredible hearing caused abundance in his life.

Snoopy illustrated powerful truths about hearing. "Then (Jesus) said to them, '**Take heed what you hear.** With the same measure you use, it will be measured to you; and **to you who hear, more will be given**. For whoever has, to him more will be given; but whoever does not have, even what he has will be taken away from him'" (Mark 4:24-25). "Therefore **take heed how you hear**. For whoever has, to him *more* will be given; and whoever does not have, even what he seems to have will be taken from him" (Luke 8:18).

Many of God's people are bound to lack and restriction because they have become dull of hearing. "For indeed the gospel was preached to us as well as to them; but the word which they heard **did not profit them**, not being mixed with faith in those who heard *it*" (Hebrews 4:2). "Mixing faith" with what we hear is not only how we get into the kingdom, but how we advance in the kingdom as well. "Did you receive the Spirit by the works of the law, or by the hearing of faith? Are you so foolish? Having begun in the Spirit, are you now being made perfect by the flesh?" (Galatians 3:2-3). When we focus more on our behavior than the hearing of faith, we reveal our reliance on ourselves and our attempt to be made perfect in the flesh.

When we prioritize intentionally hearing good news of the kingdom and mixing faith with it, we set ourselves up for great "profiting" in every area of life. We, like Snoopy, will have our ears tuned for a jangle in the Spirit to agree with. To help us walk in this "Snoopy anointing", here are four things we can do to increase the likelihood it will happen:

1. **Recognize it is New Covenant living** – As we prioritize hearing the good news of the finished work, we will stay in grace and away from a destructive works mindset. Saturating yourself in the following chapters will help you do so: Ephesians 1-3, Galatians 1-6, Romans 4-8, Colossians 1-2, Hebrews 4.

2. **Expect to hear a life-prospering word at any moment** – Expectancy is another word for faith. When we expect to hear these "jangles in the Spirit" for our lives, we will increasingly hear them (no matter who the source may be)

3. **Be excited about what you hear** – Bill Johnson, the senior leader at Bethel Church in Redding, CA, has inspired us at Bethel to respond with enthusiasm to every testimony we hear. In the same way, African American preachers often create cultures of demonstrative responses to sermons preached. These types of practices help us resist becoming dull of hearing (Hebrews 5:11)

4. **Declare what you hear** – Jesus declared Himself into victory in Matthew 4:1-11. He spoke Scriptural promises that had been made real to Him. He sets the example for us to declare God's promises over our lives

Snoopy taught me much about the power of hearing. I bless you with the Snoopy anointing!

Declarations:

1. The same way we get into God's kingdom is the same way we advance – hearing good news and believing it
2. I have an unusual ability to hear life-changing words through testimonies, sermons, prophecies, and normal conversations
3. When people encounter me, their hope levels always rise, and they are delivered from any dullness of hearing they have

# 5 Life-Changing Beliefs

*"And my God shall supply all your need according to His riches in glory by Christ Jesus."*

*- Philippians 4:19*

One of the most powerful questions to ask when facing a difficult or seemingly hopeless situation is this; What do I need to believe to have hope for this? This question will position our hearts to receive truth and to overcome the lies fueling the lack of glistening hope. We can choose to believe something different once the truth has been revealed to us. We don't declare truths to convince others, but to convince ourselves. Here are five hope-igniting beliefs:

1. **There is always a solution** – "No temptation has overtaken you except such as is common to man; but God *is* faithful, who will not allow you to be tempted beyond what you are able, but with the temptation will also make the way of escape, that you may be able to bear *it*" (I Corinthians 10:13) – There is always a solution, a way of escape. The moment we speak this, hope increases and enables us to see options and possibilities that were impossible to see in discouragement.

2. **I will always know what to do** (James 1:5-6) – "If any of you lacks wisdom, let him ask of God, who gives to all liberally and without reproach, and it will be given to him. But let him ask in faith, with no doubting..." The fear of not knowing what to do is a greater problem than not knowing what to do. Once we

ask for wisdom and believe it is coming (with the grace to do what we hear), we take an important step from uncertainty into confidence.

3. **I will thrive no matter what happens** (Philippians 4:11-13) – "I have learned in whatever state I am, to be content: I know how to be abased, and I know how to abound…I can do all things through Christ who strengthens me." Paul learned to be content. God's plan to increase our influence is to make us successful on the inside when we don't appear successful on the outside. Believing that, by Christ's strength, we will thrive no matter what happens is key to experiencing true victory.

4. **I will always have the resources I need to do what needs to be done** (Philippians 4:19) – "And my God shall supply all your need according to His riches in glory by Christ Jesus." God's provision is more than financial—He abundantly meets our needs in our emotions, protection, relationships, ideas, and more. The amount of our need is dependent on the size of our vision. If our vision is simply to pay our bills every month, our need is small. If we believe we are called to influence nations and be a great blessing to others, then our need is great and our provision will be great.

5. **My past is always turned to good** (Romans 8:28) – "And we know that all things work together for good to those who love God, to those who are the called according to His purpose." As we release our faith to this promise, God has the incredible ability to make every negative in our lives turn to a positive (whether it is something that happened to us or a poor choice we made.) This is one of the most incredible promises in the Bible.

I suggest speaking these promises out loud regularly to establish them as core beliefs in your life. They truly are life-changing.

Declarations:

1. My future is as bright as the promises of God
2. I am continually receiving greater revelation on how to activate the promises of God into my life and surroundings
3. I am one of the biggest hope-releasers in the world because I supernaturally inspire others to believe God's promises

# 4 Spiritual Reasons We Are Tired

*"But those who wait on the Lord shall renew their strength...They shall run and not be weary, They shall walk and not faint."*

*- Isaiah 40:31*

Hope for the future brings power and energy for the present. Chronic tiredness can often point to a mindset issue even more than a lack of physical rest. While our tiredness can stem from physical causes (not enough rest, being too busy, etc.), our continued lack of energy can also have spiritual roots resulting from faulty beliefs and damaging spiritual habits.

Here are four spiritual reasons we might be tired. As we respond to these, our energy will increase in dramatic ways.

1. **We Have a Religious or Perfectionist Mindset** – "The joy of the Lord is your strength" (Nehemiah 8:10). Many are tired because they do not value joy, and one root of this lack of joy is the religious mindset. This way of thinking always believes we are not measuring up and that God is mad at us. Feeling like a failure wears us out quickly, sapping our joy. Religion only celebrates and becomes joyful with perfection, while families celebrate and become joyful with progress.

2. **We Talk Frequently About How Tired We Are** – "Look at the ships...they are guided by a very small rudder...So also the tongue is a small member..." (James 3:4-5). Our words greatly

set the course of our lives. Many are tired because they regularly prophesy over themselves, "I am so tired." Certainly, we can express we are feeling tired at times but regularly proclaiming it will only help create more tiredness.

3. **We Do Not Apply Faith to Our Actions and Decisions** – For many, it is not what they are doing that is causing tiredness, but what they are believing while doing it. "Each one must give as he has decided in his heart, not reluctantly or under compulsion, for God loves a cheerful giver" (2 Corinthians 9:7). Cheerfulness is the fruit of attaching faith to the decisions and commitments we make. Faith increases energy, but reluctance and obligation are tiring.

4. **We Are Isolated from a Culture of Encouragement** – "Say to those *who are* fearful-hearted, 'Be strong, do not fear!'... Then the lame shall leap like a deer" (Isaiah 35:4-6). One key to strengthening and energizing ourselves is to give and receive encouragement. When I encounter a tired church, I almost always discover a lack of encouragement in the environment. I encourage them to make it a regular habit to take time in meetings to encourage individuals with what the team appreciates about them. If you are not in a culture of encouragement, ministries like Igniting Hope can speak words into your life to strengthen you toward the victory and influence you're called to.

"Now may the God of hope fill you...in believing that you may abound in hope by the power of the Holy Spirit" (Romans 15:13). As we believe truth, we will abound (be energized) by the power of the Holy Spirit. Let's shake off the spiritual reasons we are exhausted, and we shall renew *our* strength, run and not be weary, and walk and not faint. This sounds like a person truly abounding in hope.

Declarations:

1. I understand how to tap into the supernatural energy of God
2. I know when I am to rest and when I am not to let feelings of tiredness slow me down
3. I deliver people from the spiritual reasons they are tired

# 4 Ways to Defeat Passivity in Your Life

*"Therefore I remind you to stir up the gift of God which is in you..."*
*- 2 Timothy 1:6*

Passivity is the trait of lacking enthusiasm for, or interest in, things. It is evidenced by spiritlessness, numbness, apathy, and indifference, and is often fueled by a lack of hope. It is illustrated by the person who was given one talent in the Parable of the Talents in Matthew 25:14-30. This one did not take the risk to "arise and shine" and let the gifts and talents in him grow and impact the world. His passivity was condemned and his ending challenges us to overcome this harmful tendency. Here are four ways to do so:

1. **Stir up the gifts already in you** – "Therefore I remind you to stir up the gift of God which is in you through the laying on of my hands" (2 Timothy 1:6). "Timothy, according to the prophecies previously made concerning you, that by them you may wage the good warfare" (1 Timothy 1:18). These verses are just a small sample of the many verses which urge us to demolish apathy in our lives. Almost every morning when I wake up, I say out loud, "This is going to be a great day!" Why? Because I am attacking any tendency in me to wait to find out what kind of day it is going to be. Declarations are one of the best weapons to defeat passivity.

2. **Listen to preachers, not just teachers** – Teachers share knowledge in revelatory ways, while preachers focus on stirring

a passionate emotional response to what is being shared. We need teachers in our lives, but we also need to listen to preachers. I value people like TD Jakes, Chris Overstreet, and Mario Marillo. Their messages stir me to action.

3. **Give God something to work with** – Jesus did not create wine out of thin air in John 2. He said, "Give me those pots and put water in them." He needed something to work with. In a similar way, the Holy Spirit needed something to work with when He was hovering over "the face of the deep" in Genesis 1. "Then God said..." activated Him to bring order to disorder. As we use our gifts, as we are faithful in our assignments, and as we contribute positively into our environments, we will find God partnering with us and supernaturally multiplying what we do.

4. **Restore vision for the future** – "Brethren, I do not count myself to have apprehended; but one thing *I do,* forgetting those things which are behind and reaching forward to those things which are ahead" (Philippians 3:13). We all have "those things" to reach forward to. Vision and hope for the future gives power and purpose for the present. When we are in a prophetic culture and regularly hear who we really are and what the potential is for us, then we become motivated to be enthusiastic today, because what we do today is leading somewhere incredible. "Without a vision, the people perish" (Proverbs 28:19). All forward movement and improvements stop when there is a lack of vision, but passivity is obliterated when people lay hold of vision for the future.

Today is a good day to renounce passivity and implement these four steps.

Declarations:

1. I consistently stir up the gifts in me to reach my full potential as a person
2. I am a person full of energy, positive influence, and courage
3. I have a strong skill-set and anointing to eliminate passivity from the lives of others

# Perseverance in Promotion

*"I press toward the goal for the prize of the upward call of God in Christ Jesus"*

*- Philippians 3:14*

I love sports and have learned so much through participating in and coaching sports through the years. Athletics has the power to teach us vital character skills for life: teamwork, commitment, leadership, hard work, mental focus under pressure, overcoming adversity, dealing with defeat, finding your role within a team, and developing the ability to be coached.

Many years ago the Lord spoke to me about spiritual growth through my favorite collegiate sports team, The University of Nevada Wolf Pack. Their college football team moved to NCAA Division 1A in 1992 after a very successful stint in the lower division 1AA. Initially, after advancing to the highest NCAA competition level in collegiate football, they did not succeed as well as they had in 1AA. The better teams they played against exposed their weaknesses and shortcomings, and they started to lose much more than they had in the past. Some would say that it was a poor decision to move up to this higher level of competition because there was more apparent failure than before. After all, isn't the goal of sports (and life) never to fail or even to appear to lose? Let's just laugh at that – HA HA!

I attended a Wolf Pack football game in 2005 when they were playing Fresno State, a highly ranked team in the nation. Though Nevada was supposed to lose, they won! It was a victory that proved they belonged at this higher level of competition. As I reflected on this, I heard the Lord say to me, "Steve, I want you to lead a Division 1 life and ministry. I want you to go to a higher level and not be afraid of looking like a failure as you do."

Those who succeed most also seem to fail most. Winston Churchill said, "Success is moving from failure to failure without losing enthusiasm." As we grow into our true potential, we won't do it perfectly at first. Just as a toddler fails many times in learning to walk, we too will most likely struggle as we seek to walk in Division 1, or top-level joy, hope, heart connections, and discipline in our lives. If we do not embrace struggle as part of the process, we will lower our lifestyle and ministry down to a level that is comfortable for us and never reach our true potential.

Like the Apostle Paul, we are called and empowered to live tenaciously and courageously. "Not that I have already attained, or am already perfected; but I press on, that I may lay hold of that for which Christ Jesus has also laid hold of me. Brethren, I do not count myself to have apprehended; but one thing *I do,* forgetting those things which are behind and reaching forward to those things which are ahead, I press toward the goal for the prize of the upward call of God in Christ Jesus" (Philippians 3:12-14).

The Nevada Wolf Pack's decision to pursue a higher level has taught me not to be afraid of the process and time it takes to belong at a new, higher level. My prayer is that you too will embrace this process and any perceived failures you may experience on the journey to greater growth and maturity the Lord is calling you to. Thank you Nevada Wolf Pack for helping us see this.

Declarations:

1. I have overcome perfectionism and cause others to do so as well
2. I embrace the appearance of being a failure as I answer God's upward calls for me
3. I lean into the process in order to do what I never thought I was capable of doing

# Four Truths to Believe About Your Future

*"...He who has begun a good work in you will complete it until the day of Jesus Christ..."*

*- Philippians 1:6*

What we believe is largely going to determine what we will experience. If we only renew our minds with our experiences and our feelings, then we will most likely only repeat our experiences and emotions. With that in mind, here are some things not to believe:

- Things will only get worse
- Our prayers are not working
- We are not significant
- We don't have what it takes
- We are a victim of what others are doing
- We cannot overcome our past
- God has given up on us
- We will not be provided for

The nature of faith is to believe truths and promises higher than what we are experiencing. There will never be a convenient time to do this. I believe there are four crucial beliefs every overcomer needs to intentionally renew our minds with in order to experience great transformation.

1) **We Are Significant and Have a Significant Assignment** – As a younger leader I prayed, "Lord, I cannot wait until I can do something great for You." In response to this, I heard, "Steve,

instead of waiting to do something great, why don't you do what you are doing right now with great faith, and it will become great." This changed my life. We are all a significant part of the body of Christ, and we all have a significant assignment. As we open our eyes to it and "arise and shine" in it, we will experience purpose in a great way.

2) **We Can Do It** – The story of the twelve spies in Numbers 13 reveals that those who think they can and those who think they cannot are both right. Paul said, "I can do all things through Christ who strengthens me." A life of faith not only believes in God but believes that God in us removes all limitations off of our lives.

3) **The Kingdom is Advancing All Around Us** – One of the goals of the overcoming Christian is to see life through the promises of God and through the past prayers they have prayed. They focus on what God is doing rather than dwelling on what He appears to not be doing. They value testimonies of divine intervention and provision because they know they contain the spirit of prophecy for them (Revelation 19:10). And continuing to believe the kingdom is advancing all around us will cause us to see this advancement in greater ways.

4) **It's All Going to Be Okay** – No matter what happens, we are going to be okay (actually better than okay). We can believe this because of promises like I Corinthians 10:13, Philippians 1:6, John 16:33, John 11:25, Isaiah 54:17, and many others. Sometimes it is good to "bottom line" things and face the worst thing that can happen. As we do, God's grace will help us remove our biggest fears, and then we can build our faith from that point for the higher things that God has for us.

As we embrace these kingdom perspectives, we will increase our inner victory and positive influence. Let's believe truth and embrace hope like never before.

Declarations:

1. I have abounding hope for the future because of God's promises and His goodness
2. I believe the future will be better than the present, and I have the power to help make it so
3. I increasingly believe truths higher than my experience and my feelings

Printed in Great Britain
by Amazon

41115406R00071